The Mind and The Invisible Quest

THE MIND
AND
THE INVISIBLE QUEST

Pavan Raina

Prints Publications Pvt Ltd
New Delhi

Published by

Prints Publications Pvt Ltd
Viraj Tower-2, 4259/3, Ansari Road,
Darya Ganj, New Delhi-110002
Tel. : +91-11-45355555
Fax: +91-11-23275542
E-mail : contact@printspublications.com
Website : www.printspublications.com

First Edition : 2022 (Hardbound)

ISBN: 978-93-936743-5-7

Price: ₹ 995/-

Published and Printed by Mr. Pranav Gupta (Director) on behalf of Prints Publications Pvt Ltd, New Delhi.

REMEMBERANCE

This is in everlasting memory of our loving mother Raj Laxmi Raina (1920-2006) who will remain a guiding spirit throughout our life.

Photographs of my mother

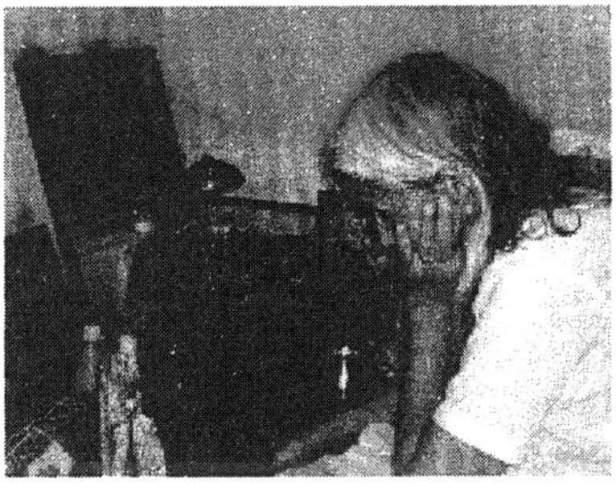

She has been very close to God devoting all her time to HIM.

Dedication

The script is dedicated to Lord *Krishna* and all the living beings who understand his power. This is also for living beings who without their knowledge inherit his power and are able to help the mankind survive by their dedicated selfless efforts on our earth, planet.

Dedication and sacrifice of such living beings have been silently guiding the path against all the odds of emerging synthetic power growing with progress of time.

- Such living beings have been keeping alive the sanctity of good and positive life.
- Such living beings would be the cause of victory of the mankind and to reach and attain the ultimate quest.

ACKNOWLEDGEMENT

My personal life has been with my small family my wife KIRTI, daughter TULIKA and son SUVEER. In my philosophical approach I may have deprived my family of many material requirements but sharing their love has only given me the strength and for that I am grateful to each one of them. All three of them have contributed enormously in my life and the process of my thinking. I would always be grateful to them.

Outside my family I would like to remember three simple people of different age group who have left a deep impact on my thought process during my early days. Mr. S. K. Kapoor (cheerful positive person) is a devoted *Krishna* disciple now, Mr. S. Batra (highly logical and practical) now settled in US with realization of east and Sameer Bhatnagar who found interest in my philosophy and his token of love in the form of a book "Autobiography of a Yogi" is able to affirm the concept which the author has generated in the book.

Preface

It is 20 years old story that the quest was generated in me to find out -

What is honesty?

What is the truth?

What is the purpose of life?

There were no simple answers but the process must have been influenced with my personal experience which can not be said of any extraordinary nature but certainly the experience must have been from a different point of view. This had prompted me to pen down the thoughts in the night ensuring the time is not disturbing anyone of the family member. Night by night the thought came in pouring as if someone is dictating to me and gradually it had shaped in some useful matter to me.

The process went for years and with the background of the subject always in the mind the amendment, addition kept happening. It was all about mind and how it must have evolved and thus made a script on the process of how human mind must have evolved and how it could be interpreted in the present scenario of the existing world. The approach was analytical and thus satisfying but the basic quest of what is truth and what is the purpose of life remained unanswered because it concerned more of 'self' and so the thinking and the writing work continued. The analysis of mental evolution in the organised social set up led to the making of my first book "The Evolving Mind And The Future World".

The theories and hypothesis generated were the useful tools for me to probe the basic unanswered quest about the purpose of life and what the honesty and the truth are to me (or anyone else)?

It is the work to extract something extraordinary from a simple ordinary experience. It is about what one views anything and how another sees the same thing and find it with differences from 0 to 180 degrees at times. It is about some simple abstract experiments which would be generating immense pleasure and peace to one whereas for other it remains attached with 'abstract' a puzzle or a joke. It is about being highly moral abiding person such that certain acts could not mean anything to others. It is about having blind trust with another human to establish an atmosphere of tranquillity between the two whereas such trust could be seen as innocence or ignorance to another. It is about sharing and showering love to all irrespective of another being of any nature.

It was not about fearing human but fearing God for any small and big step ensuring that the decision taken or act accomplished should not harm the minimum way to anyone physically, mentally, emotionally or financially. But this does not mean it must not have hurt anybody else for a simple reason that all individuals are different and one can have a control on self (if at all) and not on others. If life is like a flowing stream it has been the experience that people give importance to the big decisions in life overseeing the smaller ones which become the root cause of their problem. Naturally if simple things can not be controlled by one how could one control the larger issues? It is about behavior of a mind with another mind and the difference in the answers and the thoughts generated if the question of mind has selfish motive and if does not have one. None else is responsible for the path one has chosen and this is very rarely one believes especially if the result is not satisfactory whereas the failure in a result could be an eye opening experience for a better success in one's future course of life. In the event of a person getting a success for small or big there is a more probability to generate ego that 'I' have done it and could become a barrier in the growth of even happiness and peace unless the science of self is understood by that person.

If the self is independent body for his/her fate it is the mind which is guiding the person. The world around is real or virtual is matter of thinking. The person sees whatever is in the mind and thus makes important to know more about the mind and so ourselves. If the purpose of the author was to identify peace, contentment and the truth as a goal and mind was playing a big role it was important to unfold the functions of the mind. In doing so even mind lost its importance where higher mind was generated which we have termed as Intellect and spiritual planes and has relation with the evolutionary process as well.

The manuscript "The Invisible Quest And The Mind" is the original thought of the author and does not have any relevance present or past in his knowledge. The subjects of mind must have been thoroughly probed by different people working in varied subjects of science and psychology in different forms but author having technical background and being not a good reader in the past has not been exposed to such subjects. It is not the interest in the subject but the experience and the knowledge that could make the world look so beautiful with or without any material. The subject is about the self, the subject is about all that makes (or breaks) a self. The subject could find interest to everyone as it has ingredients to add something in their on going life which could make a difference for better. A better understanding of self could automatically add the required grains to make oneself happy, peaceful and healthy also as everything primarily is in the mind.

Mind being so important gadget in a self it has been thoroughly probed in the research by the author in this manuscript. For the explanation of the subject body it has been considered as a separate entity and the interaction of body and mind is emphasized by a hypothesis, using logical interpretation stating certain rules that are followed in and around self which can be understood by an ordinary person. Figures, graphs, and the equations are made to show that the self is dynamic and evolving and if one wants to be in the progressive path of evolution one has to know about oneself rather than the world around. The concept generated could make one aware of knowledge which one is experimenting himself or could assist in trying to have knowledge for necessary ingredient to keep one healthy or happy as the basic requirements are different for everyone and the self is in the best situation to identify. Taking a help of gurus of the master is good as a short term gain unless the process could be instrumental in activating one to understand the self for which this subject could be very useful.

If mind is understood to be controlling a self immediate quest is that who or what is controlling the mind. The analysis of the self gives that there is a superior controller than the mind which is intellect and for the explanation it becomes important to classify in different planes of mental and intellect planes. It is the plane which in isolated cases people have been reaching since long but the real knowledge to the essential mass would have relevance to the evolution and that is quite far in the time context. The study of self takes further down to this where a new spiritual plane comes in picture. Very less is detailed in the script on this subject for a simple reason that it would make the subject philosophical which is not intent.

Seeing the wonders of mind in the scientific area human has researched about nano technology on different material on one end and about the vast matter such as galaxies and stars on the other end. But the vast knowledge and the inventions to a normal human have only given an opportunity to play with their senses. The potential of self is far more that all this inventions if one can understand mind, intellect and the spiritual planes.

There are people who have roamed the world to seek the happiness and peace whereas there are people who have spent their life in a limited area. True happiness or peace has been achieved by either group and only by the people who have understood the self which is well within in the closest vicinity of anybody.

Today knowledge is increasing of the consciousness and various pundits propagate the spirituality for the peaceful end. The philosophy could be correct but it would remain a philosophy out of the bound of human to prove scientifically and so could not be of concern for a layman. The author for this reason is able to generate the concept on a self in different planes such that,

1. The primary and most important one as mental plane for which detail of the self for body and mind has been described in depth which is essential for a good health (physical and mental).

2. And then the subject has gone further from mind to the higher levels of intellect which would be the next step in the human evolution and could be understood by the explanation and the description given which lots of people (if not everyone) must have observed in their life time.

3. The last plane is spiritual plane which is a short cut from any point of evolution. Short cut to this plane gives the undisputed peace where one identifies the source of all the controller in a self.

People use the words such as consciousness, soul which is separate from the body and enable to merge with the creator whereas the author has used the word of power source fragmented in living and non-living being responsible for balancing the act to keep the total system in equilibrium in a scientific manner. How one can acquire such power with potential much more than we can think as on the day? The process has been described indicating that super persons such as *Rama* and *Krishna* have to come on the planet for the reason for balancing the loaded evil on our planet and are not any hypothetical character of an epic.

Pavan Raina

Contents

1

Creator and The Man

In this universe we definitely know a part known as earth planet with much more details than the rest. We know about one unique creation in this planet as human and much more in details about him. We know about the other world within such as animals, birds, aquatic animals, and insects and so on. We know about the nature in different form such as trees or forests, hills or mountains, rivers or sea. This man has utilized the other creatures and nature for his own advantage thinking himself to be superior species. The man himself possesses a nature which is unique of its kind and has influence on and around his life. Knowledge of anything is just the starting point and can not indicate its importance unless it is probed and experienced in details to the extent of realization. Inspite of wide knowledge gained by human in various and diverse fields and infinite mysteries uncovered he is still unaware of his own body – mind system in totality and its capability which is far more than whatever he has discovered till now putting altogether.

- The human is one creation, who can command on himself.
- He is one who can destroy the rest.
- He is one who can live on leaves, fruits and plants.
- He is one who can live on flesh and fish.

- He is one who can pass his life under the trees and one who can live in palaces.
- He is one who has developed the values; he is one who lives on emotions. He is one who has developed the comforts; he is one who lives on materials.
- He is one who has developed logic sense and applies logic; he is natural in nature and synthetic at places.

The human experience has been going since ages and would continue. He experiments on himself and experiments on others. He knows the time but with more precision about the time which is lost which is called his experience. The time changes and so the experience and in the dynamic world nothing appears constant nor the experience and it generates many questions for the continuity of his experience.

- There is a man who is keen on experiencing immediately around him. He sees and knows around him. He lives for 'Today' everyday till his last day to act.
- There is another man who sees and knows the world with different experience. He tries to enjoy the world but enjoys from 'Yesterday'.
- There is yet another type of man who sees and knows the life beyond the world. He sees the world as an oasis and life as an ocean. The ocean which appears to be endless with infinite depth. He has true clarity of high tides, he lives on 'Today' but for the welfare of mankind of Tomorrow and that is only the way he enjoys and is attracted towards the nature.

The third type of a person knows that in a definite path which is the destiny, the outcome is one that is seen at the end of road. He also knows that his path followed would guide few more others on the basis of results achieved and in turn it would help to guide others to fulfill not only their destiny but also pave a path for movement forward in mankind development. Perhaps some may think such men to be great but naturally greater would be the architect who made the *man* and the *nature* with a unique equilibrium and strong compatibility. If one component is eliminated the other would cease to exist.

The values and logics are human generation in their path of evolution and have played a significant role in overall improvement of understanding of an average person. A person experiencing and exercising a very high value life could be known as an intellectual/spiritual and could be respected by a big segment but ask him and he would say that he is still trying to know the life and knows very little about it. One may not be known (physically recognized) but still it does not prevent him to share his experience for the sake of knowing endless quest which keeps unfolding.

Higher logic has improved the living pattern of average person. The people using higher logics have been focused on their quest of knowledge and have led to various inventions. Such persons will be esteemed lot with intelligent mind but ask them about their greatness they would be humble to say that they have not done any significant work.

The big achievement (which has impacted a big sections of the world) as seen by other in either case is humbly put off as a simple task because they realize that they have spent full life for one small thing and they are further able to see the mystery beyond for which many lives would be short enough.

On the other side of the spectrum (comprising of a very large section) an average person is living a stale life or enjoying without a much sense to the others. Suffering or enjoyment of these persons prompt at sometime to know about the secrets of the life but keep wandering and elsewhere for the answer where the answer lies very much within them.

Total Harmony in the System:

Ever since the creator made the living being in our planet, He wished that the creation somehow should be able to understand Him, see Him, talk to Him and acknowledge his power to Him. Be it rivers and mountains, trees and shrubs, air or wind they follow a natural law devised for them. These living or non-living things which we can spell were provided with an ingredient of power to sustain and maintain an equilibrium in the universe. The visible earth under different internal and external conditions has different minerals and such minerals keep transforming into higher state of existence by the forces or their inherent power. It is the man's greed to swallow lower existing elements (extract) from the earth (in the form of different elements and compounds) which does not allow going to the higher state which is a far stable state in itself. A lower state of element say iron or aluminium are easily affected by the surroundings whereas the higher state of element say gold or platinum are relatively unaffected by the surroundings. Hence even in the non-living things we can see that there is a definite chemistry designed and the earth is given a power to alter its nature with the surrounding to keep the total system in harmony. Our ignorance may not allow us to understand what the total harmony is, as we do not understand the system in totality but keep altering in bits and pieces to suit our needs which keep changing with time. In the creator's design, this non-living things would contain the power and following certain set of rules for the total harmony whereas other set of existence would keep using them for their need.

There is mutual understanding between other part which also a set of power in keeping the system in equilibrium. Trees, plants, grasses are another such set in the system. It extracts specific minerals in specific conditions from the earth and has more important role to play. It makes the food for others; makes shelter for others and has mutual influence with water, air and light. Each of these ingredients has a power and a role to play in keeping the total system in equilibrium. Power of each could influence in the growth or decay of the other bodies existing such as,

- Power of air can be understood by clean fresh air, polluted air, tornado and hurricane.
- Power of water can be known by clean water, polluted water, floods and drought.
- Light or fire can enlighten or extinguish other bodies.

These substances have the power embedded by the creator but cannot acknowledge it back (at least in the knowledge of human).

Next comes the living species of animals, birds, creatures including human which are made of the above said substances of earth, water, air, fire and ether. Ether is connected with the power itself in living beings. The roles of power in these living species except human have a unique design to stay and keep the nature in harmony.

If everything lives in harmony continuously it is equal to non-existence or no development. Though different plants and creatures also evolve with time to adopt changed environment but they still live in a loop not breaking the law of disturbing the nature. It is the human which is given that extra power to break the law and to evolve to understand the creator and acknowledge him the gratitude. The breaking of a law could be a wrong word as the new entity starts following a different set of law but the power embedded in each of the living or non-living beings together have to keep the total system in equilibrium and thus human interface with the nature be the earth, sky, water, plants or other creatures keeps generating a new equations for his own survival.

It is the mind which makes the difference and ever evolving human. The evolution would continue till he understands about the power within and is capable to see and talk with the creator. The evolution of this kind is not a straight forward but is again designed with a specific law of nature by the creator.

Extinction of trees, vegetation or creatures and birth of new species for new and changed condition are the role of power in balancing the equilibrium. Annihilation and birth of bodies are the role of power. Even celestial bodies are annihilated as a law of nature and new are born. This way different types of bodies could be annihilated, get new birth but the power remains undisturbed by following its duty to keep the total harmony in the system.

It is the human and vide the route of his mind he could

know about the power, it is human who could be aware about the power which is well within and the human is following the natural law to reach there. The road to reach is torturous and most of them would keep remaining as a living piece of flesh undermining the gem that is within them to do wonders.

If the human mind is the starting point governed by a different natural law let us understand about the basic of mind and how power within us is playing the game.

The Man and the Mind

Any living being be an animal or human is a mass of body. It takes birth and passing through the different stages of age leaves the body. While he is living he is hated, he is loved and as soon as he dies the people develop a different feeling. The difference between the two states is heart and mind has stopped working. The beauty of creator here is that a moment earlier the body which was being cherished /loved /hated is difficult to hold back and is put to rest in different ways. It is not the body which was appreciated or cursed but his nature, his deeds and it is his brain which is responsible for the action. The mind is a small gadget within him that makes all the difference. The mind is the door which allows to open the view to the body and together could has enormous capability. The best way to find all about the universe and what anybody would like to achieve irrespective of his state is closest whereas one would waste his life wondering elsewhere.

Human has brain. Animals too have brain. Human is an evolving species and so there are people with different state of evolution and the difference is in the brain portion only.

What does this mean? We would know in the subsequent discussion.

There exist tribal man, rural one, urban or ultra urban man. All have brain but variance in their behavior pattern which makes the difference in living pattern. Does this mean that ultra modern man has a better brain or does the tribal men have the lower brain? If the ultimate objective of any person is to have a peaceful life and if tribal person is supposed to be in peaceful state the above statement becomes contrary and it would imply to have lesser brain and lead a peaceful life. Even if this statement is considered correct the ultra urban man can not turn to a tribal for sure and so the peace gone out from him should be assumed to be granted?

No! In fact in each category stated and also in between those categories there are people to lead successful and peaceful life. It could be their destiny but it also has significance in their behavior which they have spent knowingly or unknowingly. Thus for any existing category it is important to understand the process or the conditions responsible for a peaceful life and which could be in one's own hand.

The brain has to react with external surroundings; the brain has to react with internal happenings such as,

- A child sees his parents he reacts,
- A young boy meets a young girl both react,
- A lion enters a village the village folk react.

Also,

- She smells a rose or touches a thorn,
- He goes for trekking with natural beauty of mountains greenery.

The reaction on the brain is foremost for relating to all the external senses and is then the next step is taken. This is just one part of its function.

The body of living being is a full fledged industry with meticulously crafted machinery where every part has its unique role and has to perform non-stop. Proper food, proper nourishment, proper art for continuous functioning are again governed by the brain.

The reaction by the external senses is only the natural way and even animals do have it. Certain animals even have more intense external sense than human. This instinct among is related with its survival instinct but is not the jungle law. A dog has a strong sense for smell in the jungle and that sense continues to be even in a pet dog. Any animal does have a very special sense for its survival as a natural instinct but does not have the capability to recognize it. The man is a different animal who has recognized it and uses the animal for his strength as well. In the process of recognizing the talent of the brain the man has acquired elevated brain known as MIND.

What is mind? Is it separate from brain?

The brain is an element possessed by any living species which is responsible for its living and surviving behavior in the world. In this land, such species could have one or many inherent outstanding skills for the survival but it still allows them to live together in harmony. As soon as the living recognizes the brain in the minimum way he develops a *mind.* It would be difficult to say if it is good to have mind or not but once the mind comes in picture the natural survival instincts are changed. As soon as this animal develops a mind it opens the avenue to discover himself and the world around. This animal acquired a mind to be called as human thousand of years ago. It has been evolving since, has passed through different stages and has reached quite far but has still to cover a big distance ahead. As an early mind just coming out of brain segment he started thinking, applied and used the logic, used his organs and worked hard so as to get something more unknown. They developed the society which kept changing shape as tribal, colonial, national which were again slow processes and must have passed through many sub-stages. Today when we say that we have reached a quite advanced stage of development the quest for finding unknown still continues, the unknown thing is satisfaction and the peace which only some are lucky to realize and still fewer are lucky to achieve it. One may tend to argue that it is better not to be aware rather than incomplete knowledge about himself but the argument could only mean the person is eager to know more. Ones' *karmas* of yesterlife and yesteryears makes him reach to a place where knowledge starts unfolding for the benefit of others. The human has reached a state where the best he can do is to *think.*

Operating Bands & Operating Planes

It should be understood by the reader that the writer has used words such as brain, mind and intellect to explain the difference in the state of its being in different living being and indicates a state of being and thus the nature over one's total functioning and thus would be different from the dictionary meaning.

Mind has an impact on individual personality. Mind has an influence in surrounding also. It is thinking that has been added from the brain segment which was responsible to give shapes of the different social systems as human has adopted and continues to modify.

One may have a leadership quality while other may have a strong logic sense and mind of such individuals would not remain in isolation but have a big impact in the surroundings in a bigger growing human network. If one type of mind was instrumental in inventing material for his living comforts the other type discovered states such as love, respect, moral etc. Love and attachment were also associated with hatred and jealousy, envy sort of feelings. There is another type of feeling which has generated due to the knowledge of dependence on each other such as sense of sacrifice, having patience which is of superior outcome of the mind. Thus the development of mind and its influence around is woven by human in such a way that he cannot get away easily and so the state has come where a lot of educated people try to probe the life goal or accept that they don't know enough.

If mind in human species is supposed to command a person (himself) the organ can be classified in three segments covering the entire living species of past, present and future which form its functioning and capacity of power (Fig. 1.0). We term them as :

1- Brain band,

2- Mind band, and

3- Intellect band.

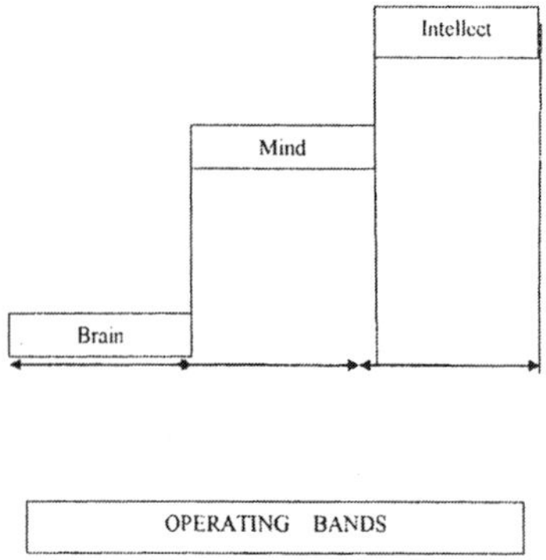

Fig.1.0 : Operating Bands

Brain band

The brain band belongs to the first stage of the development of living species. It is in all the living being except human who have outgrown from this band. This band has more pronounced interaction with external senses. It also has interaction with internal senses with a limitation. The characteristic of brain band is that the interaction is largely with the external senses and the living species is bound with natural instincts for survival for caring for their race. Perhaps species of this band could be further subdivided into three categories as,

a). Who have strong external senses such as lions and deer,

b). Who have strong internal senses such as python and lizard, and

c). Who have strong extra senses such as horse and elephant.

Different types of strength have an affect in their social pattern adopted which includes living in groups, choosing a leader of the clan, choice of food selected and so on. We could say many animals to be very talented with reference to other ones but all of them have one similarity that they belong to the brain band they keep lacking the knowledge of their skills which make them follow the natural circuitry of the cycle without disturbing the nature.

Mind band

Mind band is the higher stage. One gets by one good deed in his/her yesterlife. The mind band is an opportunity to know and understand the ruling power of the universe but before that one has to know more about the nearest body which is self. The mind band has interaction with external senses, it has interaction with internal senses and along with that it develops the thinking. The proportion of these different interacting senses differs in every individual which makes one unique. Entire human species belongs to this category and so has a great significance to all of us. Human is an evolving species and if anything that evolves is the mind and thus it is the evolving mind that is changing our world.

In this world, we see people with advantage and adverse condition, we see happy and sad people. Full of anxiety and worry on one side and completely satisfied on the other side. We see healthy, over-healthy and sick people. Can we change ourself or reduce our anxieties, worries or simply be healthy and satisfied. It could be fate to be in a state where one is situated but if one gets the knowledge from whichever source it could, it would again be a fate for the change. Fate is one thing which is not known and good to be content in absence of the knowledge on the outcome but the importance of knowledge can be gauged by the fact once he is in mind band he can not return backwards and it has the implication in his total life structure and beyond.

Intellect band

Higher developed mind is intellect. The evolution of the mind has reached a place where one can understand about such state only. This is a band where *realization* of external senses is there and so its interaction with the body is minimal. If few have reached the sun the day they would be not known or do not intend to use the leadership to attract others. It could be only due to one's individual choice and effort to live alone and be satisfied in a new feeling and could find much more comfort in elevating one step further of spirituality which is ultimate and free domain for anyone. Though spirituality is not our present subject and could be reached directly from any of the above band (which we would understand in the later part of our theory). This band is nearer to the spirituality in the path of evolution of a man. Intellect band has all the similar good and bad ingredients of the mind but with a difference. It means that love, hate, leadership, following and all other things what we would know in the mind band would be present from a different perspective. Both the bands have positive and negative elements embedded and we would understand once we have gone through the details of mind band.

If in the mind band one would be striving for power, it is the unknown quest because power comes *through* intellect stage. In intellect stage, one would be striving for superpower which would be unknown quest from the uppermost advanced band (not separately mentioned). It should be understood that there is a difference of power which intellect band could provide v/s power people try to fight for in majority of the cases. Only the word power is common but the content of power is absolutely different that we would know in the subsequent chapter.

The brain band is followed by mind band which is followed by intellect band. This is the nature's plan and the methodology to be superior and is known by different names by different people of the world. One may not be concerned even for the third band stated as intellect band as of now as human belongs to the mind band and majority among them are still in much lower part of this band.

Each band can be subdivided in sub-divisions identical in nature with difference of the knowledge and thus the total action for the similar context of any matter. The middle segment with the implication of mind is the most conflicting state which is liable to give immense pleasure to one and equally disturbed sense to the other. If we consider the first band (B) as natural state the segment three (I) could be termed of super natural state (as of now). By this definition the middle band (M) is no means an unnatural state but an important intermediate state to be understood in depth. It should also be understood that the crossing over from B band to M band could be natural design on a living being but further it is an evolutionary process (Fig. 2.0 in chapter 2).

2

Mind Band

We would try to understand the mind band by hypothetical interpretation of state and then define its function affecting one's life.

We will be using certain terms in the hypothesis which needs the clarification to the reader.

Mental Orientation

There is a difference of thinking in brain band (B), mind band (M) and intellect band (I) which results in variance of action by the living being concerned and thus the different results. Be animal or human in their respective social state could be in sound (loving) state of happiness which does not impart any negative influence to the surroundings whereas on the other side each one of these could be in an opposite (fearful) state which could disturb oneself and others as well. The difference between the two such extreme cases and all the intermediate states have the variation in *mental orientation*. Interesting mental orientation is used even for the living being in brain band.

Mental Level

As the Mind band evolves the segment of this band can be segmented in infinite small portions in the ascending order if it is stated from the lowest region. Each higher segment in this band would be in a different mental level and would be having the variation. The variation would be in their needs; variation would be in their action and so on. The living being in the brain band also could be classified in different levels but that would be brain level not the mental level.

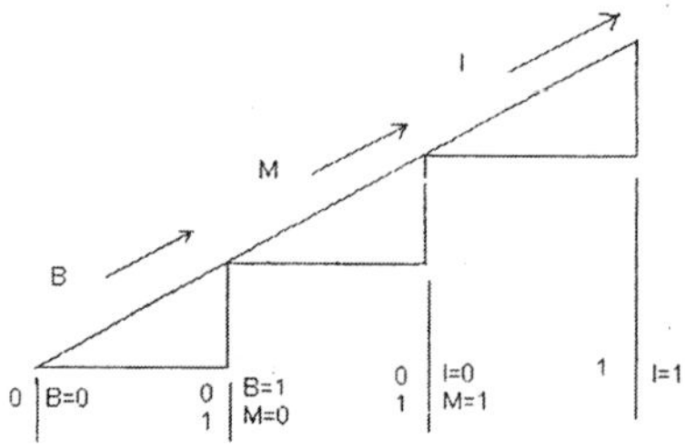

Fig. 2.0

In the brain band living species (animals) have their knowledge for physical organs and senses which they utilize as desired by the designer (God) and remain in the natural circuitry without destroying the existing balance of the nature. In the mind band (human species) the knowledge of their organs and senses has made the difference. Any improvement in the evolution further has started from the physical state of understanding. For example the apple plucked from the tree was always falling down, it still continue to fall down but Newton devised a big theory out of such physical incident. The science from this has a great significance in the advancement we have made on the day. Complex facts originate from the simpler depiction which is easier in communication and gradually leads to the unfolding of mysteries.

The role of mind is very big and is controlling many departments and functions in the body making body-mind system complete. We would hence use the diagrammatic approach to understand about the mind.

Mental Orientation

Fig. 2.1 describes the mental orientation status for living

being in brain band (State-1) and mind band (State-2).

Fig. 2.1 State-1:

Let us assume that the brain or mind is circular in shape and has innumerous lines within its outermost limit. Different lines could be responsible for different jobs assigned to it for looking after the body functioning. The pattern of these invisible lines correlates to the mental orientation. In such a case the State-1 shown is the mental orientating of the species in the brain band and the lines are concentric circles and do not change. The concentric circles ensure that the brain-body system would follow a defined pattern for living and survival and so we see that the animals follow their define traits. *We call it a natural survival behavior.*

In a natural state of brain there are all the elements to develop a mind but for its deficiency for recognizing it. The mental orientation being in a closed loop keeps them in circuit of natural instincts. This state or the instinct only teaches one what to do for its survival and is not built for challenging the superpower.

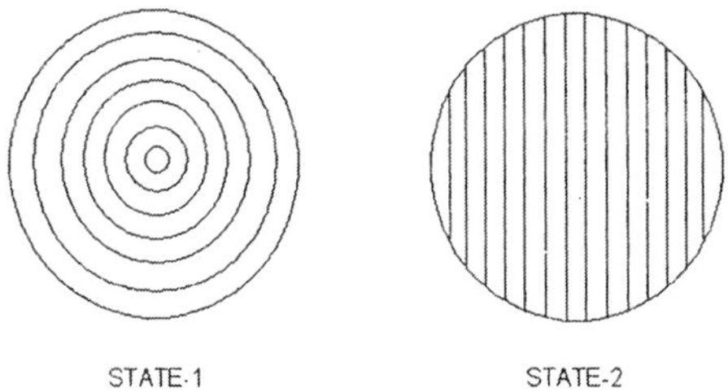

Fig. 2.1

Highly underdeveloped human in a remotely unknown uncivilized place if at all are still existing they could be very close to this condition. If animals exist in this category they do not have the knowledge of the future, do not understand long term planning and so lack the importance of time with reference to their life. What they can do best in their capacity is to utilize their external organs and senses to their fullest extent and thus have sharper reaction on their brain with their interactions.

It is God's gift to them that any and every species is provided with some positive features which it knows and utilizes as a part of its discipline. God has helped himself in the process so that he does not worry in maintaining the natural balance. If a lion is flesh eater it has a lesser regenerating capacity and if the deer is the victim to such as a flesh eater it has higher production capacity. Specific strength and its discipline only form their collective living pattern which we term as their social behavior. But for their individual, mental orientation remains the same and does not have the knowledge to interpret beyond it.

Number of hypothetical lines and the size also has significance. The size symbolizes to an extent it can grow in a lifetime of any living species. For the living being when born the size would be the space which it can grow but it starts from a very small circle with one circular ring and the rest of the space is empty. As it grows (which means as it learns the art of living) the empty space gradually starts filling but with each step of growth he encounters an endless ring which keeps confirming its behavior and thus end up having a brain with multi-circular rings. Species in this band would generally be said to have a similar brain orientation except sometime when are caught by some typical disease. In such time if the orientation is disfigured the circular lines could become slightly disfigured without loosening the end which is important to understand.

Fig. 2.1 State-2

The state shown is of mind with a space it can occupy (physically the space shown is of same size but may not have so much relevance).The parallel line indicates a sound mind with a good understanding. In the mind band such state could lead to bliss and allow to understand the correct nature of the living being including about himself. The straight line structure is an ideal stage of the living human of the highest order and with perfectly oriented state in M band. This can be understood by Fig. 2.2.

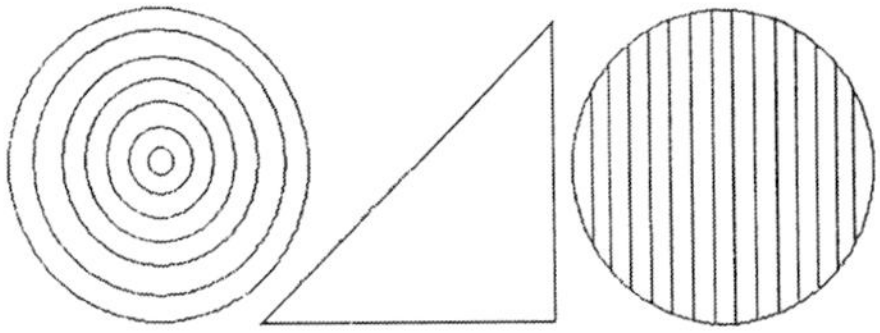

Fig. 2.2

Entire human species is covered in this band and so is important to know in more details about it. If M=0 is the state of (very early human being) when he had the minimal knowledge or when the thinking had just started. It was the state when brain recognized its form of discipline and the evolution of mind started. With the present status we have not crossed even more than the half of the distance of the travel shown as point M=1 in the fig. 2.2. In the B band the orientation was proper or disturbed in very specific instances whereas in M band orientation varies from symmetric to extremely asymmetric and its nature varies at different position of the travel between M=0 to M=1.

Mental Level

Mental level is the position of a human situated in M=0 to M=1. The different mental level has different pattern of requirement for his body and for its proper functioning. We have also stated that the present human has not crossed the midway that is M=0.5 and thus has to cross a big road in its mental evolution. Let us see the basics of how mind at M=0 is different from the brain which would throw the light on evolution of mind. The mental level can not be separated here for understanding the mental orientation in the mind band.

Once the mind band enters from the brain band the circular (endless) loop is cut. In the beginning the cut could have been in one or few lines of the infinite circles and gradually with time and with generation ahead the cut could have been apparent in all lines as shown in fig. 2.3. This situation he would have been very uncivilized but with a distinct knowledge to form a social group to confront the wildest beast. As the mental level rises the cuts in the loop increases, the lines get widened up. The widening up has to evolve to become straight line pattern as shown in fig. 2.2 State-2.

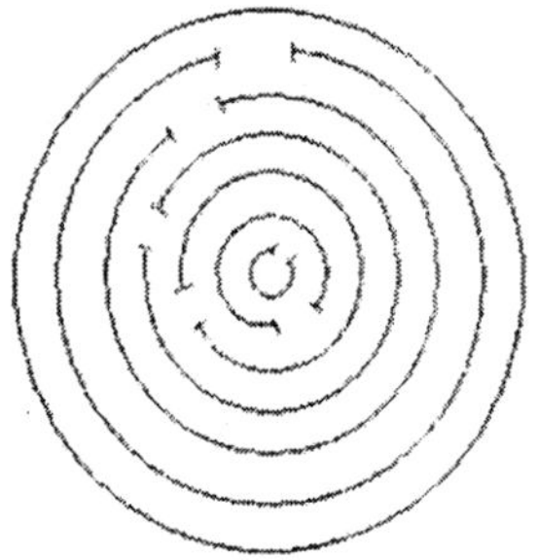

Fig. 2.3

M=0 is a state where brain ceases to exist in its original form. There is a break in the circular loop of its brain orientation to be in the natural way. This is a significant change and once loop is broken it can not be repaired to the original form. This phenomenon means the break in harmonious living with only natural instincts. The cut off point is where dependence on his external surroundings resulting equilibrium with the internal body system, ceases to be complete as it was earlier but there is something more responsible for the system to be in equilibrium.

May be the definition of human starts from this point, may be this human is proud of himself but probably he does not know what good it is for him to be human and what good he can do for others or even for himself. It should be understood that the slot generated in the circular loops is because of the addition of something which is the power to *THINK* and once it has developed it is an irreversible habit for the entire species to come ahead.

Mental rise is the part of evolving mind and we have to cross over the big journey but the mental orientation is a state applicable in all the mental levels. The orientation at any level could be of either symmetric pattern or asymmetric pattern.

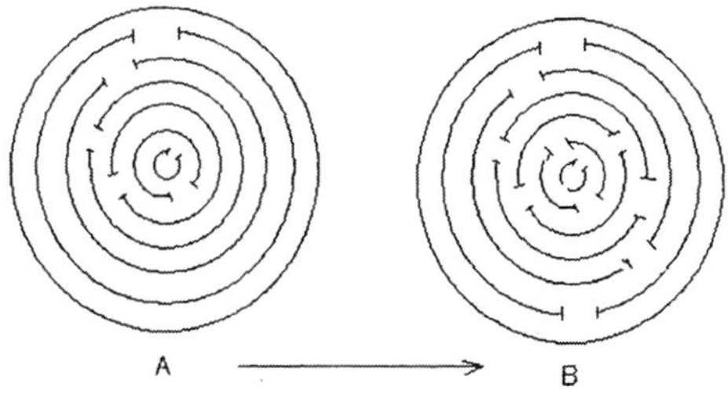

Fig. 2.4

Once the power of thinking has entered with passage of generation and time there has been the changes in the hypothetical lines drawn in the mind. If the cut in the loop (fig. 2.4A) was the first point the human developed that allowed to develop some social format and applied minimum logic for their survival beyond natural way existing. Then there was another cut in the loop as seen in the fig.2.4B. Once both the ends were open, mind had sharpened. He was gaining the knowledge from a different perspective but was still an uncivilized person. Now his logics improve. The mind and thus the human is becoming more knowledgeable to what the early human had been in the starting point but gradually the situation is also becoming complex as shown in the fig.2.5.

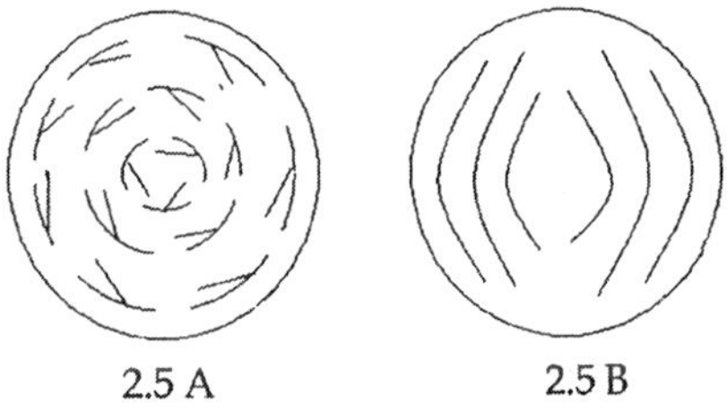

Fig. 2.5

The figure above shows the extreme case of the mind where at one end (fig. 2.5 A) it has become complex and on the other side (fig. 2.5 B) it has become superior.

The break in the loops and widening process can alter the orientation with understanding or misunderstanding of the social norms and values so termed and which show as a reaction in the social to others. The opened loops could be more complex than fig. 2.5 A or more refined than fig. 2.5 B in the above diagram. Situation A is extreme case of asymmetric orientated mind and it would create all sorts of anxiety, fear like things in self. It could lead to a state of turmoil within oneself and the surrounding and would emit the negativity of all kinds.

The situation fig.2.5 B is of a symmetric mind with proper mental orientation. This state would have the tendency to bring a peaceful surrounding within oneself and around. Once the person has the mental level above 0, (M=0) he could have extreme case of mental orientation at any age of the time. If the mind is evolving at every stage of evolution there are minds which are dividing the course of their path by keeping mental orientation in symmetric condition or asymmetric condition. If the asymmetric condition causes the negativity the influence by such state of mind at higher mental level is much higher.

These orientations are not mere fixed lines. They vary from time to time and in any part of the day. Any specific person of any age could have an average range of variation that *could lead to the generation of a very different nature in that person*. It is that person the best judge who is capable to evaluate his state and can try to orient the mind which would mean many things together such as living a healthy life, helpful in nature and constructive behavior. It would also mean the elevation of the prominently noticeable mental level and thus influencing the surrounding towards the positive side.

Body and Mind

It is important to know the coordination and inter-dependence of body and mind on each other resulting in the nature of an individual personality. The effect of individual nature does have impact on surrounding influencing many more minds and thus bodies.

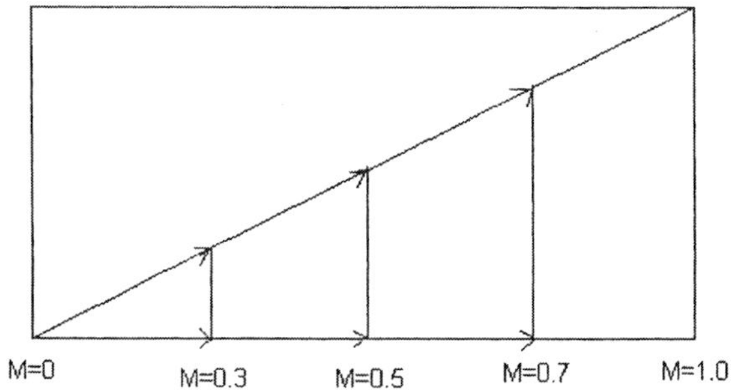

Fig. 2.6

M=0 is the staring point of human knowing their skills beyond natural instincts. Crossing this point the mental evolution, it has to ascend in the process of growing as in Fig. 2.6. The rise is inevitable but even after so many thousands of years the rise has not exceeded very far from the stated mark of M=0.5. What we understand by this?

1. Mental rise would mean different nature of living being (as in this case the nature of human being) with different qualities in interdependence with the individual bodies and thus the difference in the results on individuals. The ultimate effect is far more and is not restricted to individual and spreads in the larger associated society.
2. The average mental level has not increased beyond M=0.5 as stated but the evolving individuals have climbed further also. The tiresome effort of individuals allows climbing up the ladder but the acceptance by mass is not an easy task and takes enormous time to change its location.

At M=0 level is the highest level where the animals who have special skill for survival could exist and it is still the state where living is the "art for survival" and whatever it does is the activities using the organs and senses physically. As soon as the living being rises above this, it is not that he thinks to do less physical effort but he ought to do it.

Mental level is a state acquired by ones *karmas* and means to acquire the skill through which the living being would climb up the ladder to reach maximum of M=1.0.

Before we understand the complexity of mind let us see one basic simple law in the Fig. 2.7.

We take the advantage of the word mental orientation as a tool.

Further we can use a momentary mental orientation as a state where one feels the satisfaction with or without one's knowledge.

At M=0 state the living being is stated in perfect mental orientation with P=1.

P signifies the physical energy which is consumed by using physical organs and senses. Such species could utilize only physical energy to be in the natural circuit. The orientation in them is perfect when in peace and could be said disturbed in the distressing condition.

Step further from M=0 the physical energy does not remain good enough for mental orientation where one more variable is added as mental energy signified by the word M.

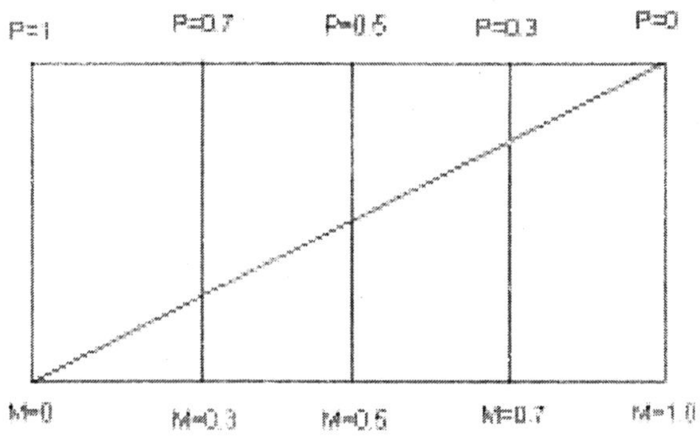

Fig. 2.7

Satisfaction

How the satisfaction can be defined?

Feeling of satisfaction is a mental state where the sum of physical energy and mental energy remains constant and is equal to unity.

If S stands for satisfaction,

P stands for physical energy and

M stands for mental energy.

The satisfaction (S) at M=0 demands physical energy=1 and mental energy=0.

Therefore satisfaction equation is

$$S = P + M = 1 + 0 = 1.$$

Mental level in a state of rise is the path of mental evolution and one attains by his own *karmas* and is located where one can apply his skills to climb up the ladder. For climbing up the ladder of mental plane for even a fraction it is important that one should have symmetric mental orientation. It is very difficult for human being to keep the mental orientation always in the symmetric mode and thus one has to understand and try to keep near to such state most of the time and for that again one needs the knowledge. For the basic knowledge one should consider satisfaction as a primary goal on day to day basis and the primary goal can be applied by balancing a simple equation for satisfaction.

For this, one has to identify the location where one is situated in the mental level graph of M=0 and M=1 as a tool. For the total understanding following points would help in locating oneself.

- For ease of understanding the graph has been subdivided into four important landmarks as 0.3 M, 0.5 M, 0.7 M and 1.0 M.
- It should also be understood that before the M (Mind) plane, lies B (Brain) plane and beyond M (Mind) plane lies another I (Intellect) plane.
- The average evolved human has barely crossed 0.5 M

level with many unrecognized human much higher in the level.

- Human below 0.5 M level are prone to be influenced by the B plane whereas crossing 0.5 M one could get influenced by the I plane.
- Situated in higher mental level does not make one superior. 0.5 M person is not superior to 0.3 M. Infact one rises to lift others and a true symmetric oriented person at higher mental level would know this.

The objective should be not to get influenced by either plane and to understand where one is located and derive day-to-day satisfaction which would automatically give the knowledge and lift oneself.

A person could be at 0.1 M level or 0.4 M level. For deriving day- to-day satisfaction both have to fulfill the energy equation of unity.

Person at 0.1 M level one could derive satisfaction by

$$S = P + M = 1 = 0.9\ (P) + 0.1\ (M)$$

Whereas person at 0.4 M level one could derive satisfaction by

$$S = P + M = 1 = 0.6\ (P) + 0.4\ (M)$$

It is the physical energy and mental energy combination that is being utilized, governs the satisfaction. According to the law a person lying at 0.1 M has to invest more in physical energy and less in mental energy whereas a person at 0.4 M level has to put lesser physical work and more mental work. This energy being relative has to be gauged by one own reference.

In the mind-body system it is basically the mind which is controlling the entire functioning of system. In absence of knowledge one tends to over strain or under utilizes and consequently faces different types of problems.

Referring the Fig. 2.7

i. At 0.3 M level has capability to have the knowledge of the body (organ and sense).

ii. At 0.5 M level he is aware about the body with more understanding of the power of mind.

iii. At 0.7 M level is a critical stage where one starts getting the knowledge for the actual mind and consequently starts realizing about the organ and senses. One starts knowing the power of mind.

iv. At 1.0 M power of mind is known. This stage would give a new joy and all the knowledge gained till now may appear to be of least worth.

The last point could not be of much significance to the larger society as on the day because of their reach but still it is good to understand the impact. Any point above 1.0 M would mean stepping into new (I) intellect band where you don't loose what you have learned but the definitions of simple logics and the values begins to have a meaning with a difference and so the thinking and action tends to alter but the self has to start acquiring the knowledge once again. Nevertheless the beginning is from a different level and so it is with newer energy and newer power of body and *Intellect* than the *mind.*

The knowledge of satisfaction is associated with happiness and pleasure like feelings for which a person starts running but he neither knows the source to achieve it nor does he have the parameter to measure. To answer this question it is important to know that it is his body and the mind which is responsible and it is his body and mind which have the measuring parameters inbuilt. The poor person wanders in wilderness throughout the life in absence of the knowledge of his own constitution and the ability.

A human living being irrespective of his mental location has to have symmetric mental orientation for feeling of satisfaction. It can be seen from another side that when one feels satisfied he is having a symmetric mental orientation at that moment which could help to track back the event for the result to avoid from the illusion what the most suffer from. There could be situation of person existing in the lower mental level and has enough of material comfort. He avoids putting enough of the physical efforts and does not fulfill the equation for satisfaction, creates asymmetric mental orientation and thus makes him unsatisfied. There could be a reverse situation for a person lying in a higher mental level has to undergo much harsh physical efforts for survival (which could be attributed for his *karmas*) which would create asymmetric mental orientation.

Mind is a state which gives an opportunity to realize about the body, organs and senses. Any person who masters any of his organs and or senses and utilizes his experience as a habit could move towards the realization and thus fulfilling the equation of satisfaction (S = P + M = 1).

Probably many of the human of different levels would be reaching the state of realization and understanding the contentment (as a real satisfaction) towards the very end of their lives. They would know that the life is nothing but the survival art with their own experience but for the same end result (unknown earlier). Such person and their experience could not necessarily help others to realise it in the same way.

For example Ram gets a king of fruits, an alphanso mango which also turns out to be very delicious. He can communicate about its richness of the taste to Sham, he can emphasis it but can not make other realize about it. On the other side Sham gets a similar alphanso mango which tastes similar but Sham finds nothing so special to admire about it. Ram with symmetric orientation might have with a sharper sense of taste organs whereas Sham with asymmetric orientation might not have liked as he had a much higher (over) expectation within him to create doubt.

Influence on Body and Mind

The satisfaction equation of unity (S = P + M = 1) explained is a primary law applicable throughout the life and lives to come. The law helps for making the mental orientation symmetric and thus to elevate the mental level which are two different things in any person of any age and any time. The equation, P + M explained in not merely a combination of external body and mind but needs more knowledge influencing the system. Mind band is influenced by three things,

1. External body organs and senses: Relates to the action and interaction of external body, organs and senses with surrounding. Few examples such as plucking of fruits, smelling a scent, running after a ball or even getting wet in the rain. We will be using a term **BOS** (body, organ and senses) for this activity further in the essay.

2. Internal body senses: Relates to the requirement of body which a person needs and also the art of converting the intake into required chemicals for running the system. We would be using a term **IBC** (internal body chemistry) further for this activity. IBC has a great significance to understand as the capability of mind in the extreme case is to generate nectar or poison from the same ingredient with the status of other parameters involved. Great *Meera* the devotee of *Krishna* had to consume the poison by force which got converted into nectar, one might think this to be a mythological story but that is the actual power and the ability of the highest order.

3. Mental Synthesis: Relates to the knowledge generated in human being as thinking. The thinking has further added feelings like love, hate etc. and differentiate as human. We would be using a term **MS** (Mental Synthesis) here onwards. Mental Synthesis has a direct and indirect reaction on the other two elements of BOS and IBC and thus on the body – mind system overall.

Referring Fig. 2.7 the landmark for the three elements of BOS, IBC and MS and its importance is as below,

i. M=0: The beginning of THINK TANK and breaking the natural circuit behavior.

ii. M=0.3: Knowledge of BOS.

iii. M=0.5: Knowledge of IBC and realization of BOS.

iv. M=0.7: Knowledge of MS and realization of IBC.

v. M=1.0: Realization of MS.

The result of our life is the cause of our actions. The action and interaction has an effect on all the three elements. The inter-relation among them exist always irrespective it is in our knowledge or not. For gaining the knowledge at any mental level if, satisfaction equation is important tool and for the state of symmetric mental orientation, basic need is the prime mover of the system.

Basic Elements Linked with the Mind

The mind is governing three elements (BOS, IBC and MS) simultaneously in the path of rise whereas mind is being governed by the person where there is stagnation in the rise of mental level. Let us know the interdependency of some basic traits of survival and the mind.

The basic traits are those present in any form of living being and generally are in the following order,

i. primary basic need is the food,

ii. secondary need is the shelter, and

iii. third need is sex.

Food and the mind

The trees and plants are also aware of their basic requirements for their survival. Any soil, any nutrients and any climate can not grow any plant. Each species of plants is defined to flourish in a specific situation. The plant or the tree also has to give the value to the other living being in natural chain defined by a super power.

Next in the brain category animals exist and they very nicely know their needs. There are grass eaters, plant eaters, flesh eaters and so on. The trees, grass or the flesh is available in their approach area for their survival which is again the mapping done by the super power. The super power has imbedded the dependence of basic need (food) with the three elements in their category where they operate without their knowledge but for the benefit of the rest. In the brain–body segment there is a gradation in the natural behavior and natural instinct which can be judged in their diet.

- A pig for instance is situated at the bottom most ladder in brain segment and has a beauty in its IBC coordination is that the pig would eat all the rubbish and garbage for others but is capable to extract and convert into useful matter to survive. The animal cleans the environment at the cost of self whereas higher animals' do not hesitate in eating his flesh. It stays in the filth but survives inspite of it. Its brain-body system is so poor that it does not even know to turn back swiftly. If the situation arises, it runs forward only. There is nothing to pity as it is a creative and definite design of the creatures to keep the entire system in natural balance.
- An elephant which would come in one of the highest order in the brain segment is strict vegetarian. Its vegetarian diet has generated a sixth sense and is able to communicate with their kith and kins separated out of their visible limits. Having a powerful does not kill others.
- There are animals who are aware of specific leaves or grass or salts available in their land which they consume as a medicine for controlling their IBC.

With mind band coming in picture the scenario is not so simple because of the added variable in his being. The same human at different mental level needs a different food habits.

But does he know?

The changed food habit is responsible to influence the MS and in turn has the capability to tune IBC. As one rises in the mental level his physical need (energy) is reduced and in symmetric orientated condition the food requirement becomes refined.

If at or before level M=0 the human was able to digest even raw flesh and crude fruits and leaves. It changed further with baked flesh and vegetables and then cooked ones and so on. Once mind has come in the picture he starts knowing about the external organs (BOS) but is unable to see the IBC which has equal role in his total development. The mind at a particular level has to perform for controlling BOS, IBC and

MS together for the total growth. Mind has to instruct the external organs for any action.

For example, say for holding a pen, mind has instruct hand to take to the place where pen is kept and do the necessary action of hands and fingers to hold it.

Likewise there are infinite internal organs and it has to instruct each of the organs for their duty to accomplish the total action. The mind has to direct the internal organs to produce different types and proportions of chemicals for the smooth running of the system. The mind also has to use its data bank and its logic and values learned along with the data and the analysis which would make him aware of such things.

For example, when a human sleeps the logic and the data of human (MS) part have diagnosed that a chemical is produced known as barbiturates. Scientists have thus produced synthetic barbiturate (e.g. calmpose) which induces the sleep in the patient. The mind in a normal situation instructs internal organs responsible for the production of calmpose *sort* of chemical so that the person sleeps when tired. We do not yet know the capability of the mind and would be restricted by certain knowledge that has been discovered. For inducing the sleep itself different people at different mental levels would be requiring different sets of chemicals in different ratios.

Would we ever know all these finer details?

Our knowledge would always be way behind its capability which it is already performing. The best is to keep a symmetric mind and rest it would do itself.

Similarly there are infinite internal organs which are doing its job good or bad and if they are not properly functioning it is oneself responsible rather than anybody else. For another instance, we consider a stomach which is the receiver of the food taken. The stomach is an area where food is processed with operation like grinding, dissolution, extraction for ease of further processing into vital components for the body and mind. For this to happen different chemicals or the combination of chemicals are generated for which mind has the major role to play. The mind is responsible to think and know and with each rise in step of mental level has the capability to adjust and fine tune IBC and BOS such that it has residual time to think and plan further.

But do we know at all about our mind?

Or do we only burden it to trouble ourselves. Improper functioning of IBC could be identified as some minor upset and that individual would be the best person to know the solution whereas in the present world he does not have the time to understand and leave on others.

The food is the basic need for the body-mind functioning. If only food was not essential the whole evolutionary process would have been different. We still do not know what our body requirement is and it is oneself only responsible rather than anybody else about himself. One has not to go in libraries or to the teachers essentially for such knowledge. Entire knowledge is stored in the mind and with general awareness of knowledge whatever one has acquired in the due course as his experienced in his life in his own way is enough. The life is continuous, the experience is continuous too, the infinite capability of the mind would keep opening towards the mysteriously and astonishing direction only if there is minimum desire in oneself. If one has never thought and tried and has been slave of unwanted portion of his own, he would be troubling his own body and the cause would be some of the ailments. The aim here is to generate the gate for the basic knowledge where every individual could find its own requirement oneself.

A good tasty food for an Indian villager, an urban modern Indian and a western person could be different as they all would be of different mental level (generally but not necessarily). It is not the method of cooking or decoration which differs but the nutrition, food value and the digestibility of the food. If scientists are growing and creating the hybrid fruits and vegetables it could be their realization as the food for human in the ages to come of people of still higher mental level.

The Fate

There is always an element of fate involved for the human living. Human birth itself is a fate and is associated when one is born. The pure mind is larger and has the capability to overcome the limitation if any by fate of situation and cross over to a much higher level. Let us take the example of food habit for this.

In the growing synthetic world a person situated at lower mental level may be growing the eatable in the field or could be able to afford the luxury of any food. He comes to know the art of cooking which is suitable of higher mental level without his knowledge about it. He relishes the food and has a habit of it. Such person if has symmetric mental orientation because of the situation would in most probable condition tend to rise in the mental ladder. Whereas on the other side a person lying in the higher mental level could be having the limitation where either cannot afford the food he knows would suit him or unknowingly gets the adulterated food which tends to stagnate the mental growth. The situation could be said due to his fate. The fate here is used as this human has the knowledge about the need but the situation prevents him. In such situation his knowledge could work and mind would allow doing re-adjustments for balancing BOS, IBC and MS. Either he adjusts by S equation and does more physical work than what he should require as a natural wish to keep his mental orientation symmetric or lesser down the burden on mind, on external organs and senses so that he can make up the thinking power. The later proposition would amount to go one step ahead in the mental level where there would be a better control on external senses.

And the Capability of Mind

A human being might belong to any mental level and with any food habits and living style but his mind knows exactly what is required for the body and how much is needed. In S equation physical and mental energy proportion are not an absolute figure and in a situation when any part of the external organs has worked more (BOS) or more mental thinking (MS) was there for a specific IBC to cause deficiency in the body the knowledge for symmetric orientation mind would indicate the BOS about the present requirement.

Example, a symmetric oriented mind would indicate eye for the selection of food, tongue to eat sour, sweet or salty whichever is required at that time. The beauty of the mind and symmetric oriented state is that it has capability to dilute the scientifically known fact in terms of vitamin, proteins etc. such the mind could find out the ingredient within ones available and affordable state. The body requires so little whereas an asymmetric mental state would overeact and could make one eat anything for unbalancing BOS, IBC and MS and appearing as disorders of different kinds.

Ironically the human today is facing the primary problem in this area of basic need itself. If one is rich enough to afford any kind of food he has a problem and if one thinks he can not afford he has a problem. Both the sections would be affording some food if not the best (as they think) and that available food could be good enough to promote their satisfaction, to rise above in mental level doing which could change their meaning of living with a greater purpose of the human community.

- What generally is happening is that one is enjoying the food which he knows is delicious giving importance and unwanted burden to the tongue and depriving himself from understanding the instruction from the mind or realizing for his requirement in the end of the day (overuse of BOS).
- It could be that one is so busy that he does not have the time to think on food, he does not find time either to think what is delicious or even his mind. He eats because it is essential and could gulp anything without a serious thought on the mind which is involved in other worldly matters (Overuse of MS).
- There could be another person who can not afford the best food and thinks that what he can afford is not good

enough and thus is killing himself. (Under utilization of BOS).

What do we mean by over use and under utilization of BOS?

In the above example, it is asymmetric mental state (at that moment of meal) when a person is imposing his organs to react than to work with his mind.

- His eyes are trying to judge the taste,
- His tongue is trying to relish and
- Hands are equally trying to contribute their part.

We are burdening the organs what they are not capable of and not using the mind which is the correct tool.

What is required before starting the meal is,

- To bring the mental state in symmetric orientation or closest possible,
- Temporarily allow the mind to see the meal,
- Allow the mind to feel the food,
- Allow the mind to taste the food.

If mind uses the organs for their respective work and takes the vital decision itself a person would enjoy the meal, he would have only as much required and select what is proper for his system to remove the deficiency bringing the harmony between BOS, IBC and MS.

This could appear hypothetical but anyone and everyone can practice and become intelligent.

Shelter and the mind

Shelter is second most important in the race for survival and comes out of the natural instinct. It is important for survival and the species has to select the location and method and for that they identify their strength of BOS and opt for it. This is applicable in the species in Brain band as well. The shelter is safeguarding oneself from the external conditions from the predator or the nature's fury of weather,

- A lion might select an open area below a hill. His body

is able to withstand the wind and storm and has no apparent fear of other animals.

- Bison or dear stay in huge flocks which is their best weapon. Some are lost as a prey but they get the strength in collective to keep living in such fashion.
- Some smaller creatures / animals stay in the burrows and the holes made in the hillock or in the ground.
- Chimpanzee stays on the trees, make branches and leaves as their cozy bed. They also use large leaves as umbrella to safeguard from heavy showers.
- And so on...

In the human kingdom the mind has come in the picture and MS has generated the ego that I am superior to those animals and thus taken him away for the natural method for shelter. With MS emerging to the minimum degree it has dependence with BOS and IBC resulting to finds a solution to prevent his body from the external surroundings. It is now that the wind, dust, hot or cold or other varying natural conditions starts bothering him. At lower mental level his body is capable to withstand much rough conditions because he is in the zone of utilizing high physical energy but as soon as he starts climbing upwards the tolerance level starts declining. He does not want his mind to pain on body and tends to prevent from such rough living and starts finding the comfort.

With mental level rising his living habit also needs to re-adjusted. He requires cleaner and hygienic conditions with his interacting surroundings. With this elementary knowledge people have made big bungalows and air-conditioning like gadgets for the comfort.

Do these gadgets aid him really?

It is true that human has to prevent himself from the external natural condition of any mental level existing today but are these modern materials for comfort absolutely essential where a very small quantum of people in the world could afford it.

What would one do who stay in a hut, where dust and storm

are frequent?

To answer this we have to understand the social format made by human where there is a difference between the leader and the follower. In a true sense a leader or could be in a positive way be said a teacher or a guide (who is supposed to be in higher mental level) would invest his energy with the people and as much less time for himself. If one has to run / work for 20 hrs a day a short nap in a cozy controlled atmosphere does make a sense. The material developed could aid him which still does not is of his prime concern. He has to take a short rest and start again for the march with the people. It is his MS which is active controlling his nature and the movement and it is the people who have provided the comfort for the best returns to them.

On the other side if one can afford the best material, by any chance which is not a bad thing it could be his *karmas* giving him the opportunity but the utilization of BOS, IBC and MS remains at the top. In such a case if he is not utilizing the best of his available resources the best comfort would start giving all the problems.

The advanced material comfort has helped human to make their dwelling which otherwise could not have been possible. In a very cold country where icy winds keep blowing proper enclosure and condition becomes very important but comforts don't work as substitute for the mind elements. Living with minimum or maximum comforts is not the primary concern for a person who is balancing the mind with the three elements of BOS, IBC and MS. In the case of easy availability of material if one is underutilizing any of these components it would surface out in his nature external or internal. He could have agitating nature, disturbing attitude affecting others or would suffer from physical or mental disorder and so on.

There is always a part of the fate which could be prominent. Minimum condition of shelter is required for survival. If one has made a hut near the river side or the sea shore and if a big tide or the floods washes away the hut along with the living being it could be a fate but there are other who have taken the birth to help such lot. The mind is a wonderful piece of element and has a capability much beyond the expectation and one's knowledge.

Two identical healthy looking persons if are made to stand in open where the temperature is 22°C wearing equal amount of clothing and are asked how are they feeling? One could even shiver and ask for clothing protection whereas the other could feel good. It is the combination of their mental level and the momentary mental state which is responsible. If this can be understood why would not everyone try to have the state as the later case even in the difficult condition? Material comforts are not bad at all but mind never says I need a bungalow; I need an air-conditioner and so on.

A person situated at 0.3 M level is able to adjust his mind elements and is able to keep the mental orientation symmetric in the adverse condition of surrounding atmosphere the mind would try to elevate higher say 0.4 M and thus give that a person an opportunity for the growth. At the higher platform definitely he would have much higher level of realization of BOS and the surrounding would reduce hurting him. This is a tedious task nevertheless not impossible. If considered as an opportunity it would lead to a far satisfying end than what the S word stands for in our equation.

The best of living style could be giving the physical comfort and also generating physical fears and so unless the potential of mind is harnessed the true meaning of comfort is difficult to understand. The simple primary rule remains the same of following the equation S and understanding about the mind elements with oneself.

Sex and the mind

One believes or not there is a superpower who has crafted the entire creation without a slightest flaw. We human being before knowing and believing such a notion have to understand our ownself and then rest would follow itself.

How great is the relation of body and mind that if mind

has enabled to give the knowledge of his external organs and senses which it was already utilizing by the knowledge of natural instincts. It has also enabled him to think and act affectively for the comfort of his three elements of BOS, IBC and MS.

The mental synthesis (MS) has added the word like comforts in his life and thus allowed him to give the knowledge of pleasure. There are people with half baked knowledge of pleasure who run after it with different needs and different results. Some may spend their full life effort for pleasure and comfort and still in the end might find not reaching near it whereas other inspite of the best effort towards it could feel deriving the pleasure.

Man could be using varying degree of material for achieving pleasure and comfort. He could be also drawing his own line of comparison for achievement to feel happy or distress. The fluctuating desires generated in the process could harm in search of something more than one has achieved in actual. Pleasure and comfort are like oasis which gives an illusion from a distance. Go near it there is not fun and no excitement but not to all, not to those who understand the mind.

The question now generated is that if comfort and pleasure are the elements emerged from the MS portion of mind what is measuring parameter. It is important to understand what the limit is and what is beyond. It should be understood that MS has emerged from his mind within oneself and thus the reference point also lie within oneself and nowhere else. The knowledge and the realization for parameters of comforts and pleasure are embedded within him and emerge from sex.

Sex is a vast word and the easiest one to be carried away. For the species in the brain band it is the tool for running the race. It is the regenerating act given by the superpower and emerges in some specific conducive period. Every species undergo the act for they are bound in the natural instinct and cannot think beyond. Even in the brain band it comprises a pleasure for which they even fight to death at times but is far from their knowledge. Naturally why should a female bear the burden and the pain and why should male opt for mate at all if some pleasure is not there. It is truly associated with some unknown element which starts unfolding above M=0 level.

Sex is the process which gives the indication to the body-mind system about the parameter and the limitation which could be used as a tool for the mental rise. It is the process which gives the highest order of pleasure but is for the shortest time interval. The basic pleasure which the mind has desired from his body could be met probably by other resources as well.

In the natural instinct the act of sex could be seen as a secondary in nature after food and shelter but in actual one might be getting a chance whereas the other being deprived of it. In this segment when the urge is generated for the sex in the brain the body does not know anything and the result inside the body (IBC) is the poisonous situation. There are two aspects for the creator to make it important,

i. If male-female element and the sex with derivation of pleasure was not there the cycle of any species would not have been continued and so the essence of such writing would not have been there.

ii. It was also the method by which the creator of nature has assured his berth and the superiority.

Whereas God has ensured the balance of the system by the nature of the act. He has also given one additional tool to the human to understand the realization for going up in the ladder of mental level. In the mind band sex is responsible for the best and also the worst. The first human value ever generated in the process of his mental evolution was *love* which remains the most important. Elevation of aesthetic sense has come by covering the sex organs in the beginning and it had changed the meaning of sex and it was not a mere tool to run the race. The love ingredient with the larger meaning has allowed developing the knowledge of unknown element of pleasure in different forms and habits. Not to forget that it was the love responsible to make him *human* and responsible for all the discoveries and invention related to scientific and value with progress of time.

How does the mind see the sex? It is essentially a natural ingredient at all levels of brain and mind. We would see that mind (active mind as would be seen in the next chapter) has no place for sex and is negative in nature. The mind does not see anything bad but simultaneously knows the limit to use it and never sees as the end.

Sex and satisfaction equation

Why does sex give pleasure? We have explained in the satisfaction equation and the symmetric mental orientation earlier. We know that equation physical and mental energy should be one for achieving the satisfaction. The act of sex has such a beautiful blend of both the energy to give the pleasure and thus satisfaction. The pleasure is experienced by the mind by the help of the body. The act of sex also helps to orient the mind but very temporarily. The mind also has to cater the need of IBC and MS an asymmetric oriented mind might never know the excess of pleasure causing the imbalance within a trio BOS, IBC and MS and thus the mind. In the asymmetric oriented mind it is his incorrect knowledge about pleasure and the comfort which creates the urge to acquire more and more with reference to BOS only. Such person might want to continue his eye to be pleased with sex, his hand to feel, his tongue to taste and so on.

He does not want to know that the pleasure is momentary state and the mind within does not sleep and thus the momentary break would help in making mental state symmetric. A mind can be symmetric only when it is capable to think and realize about him. On the other hand if a glimpse of power could be enough for realization a momentary pleasure could help him to realize to work for the real un-harming pleasure.

Pleasure and mental level

Refer fig. 2.7

We have different landmarks at different stages of mental evolution. Sex has been from the beginning. Love value emerged from it and enabled to give a shape of society for the progress. The unknowing unsaid pleasure had been there in sex since inception of any species. Mind enabled to give the knowledge of pleasure. The knowledge at different level starts unfolding more and more mysteries which become part and parcel of the society when there is an added value and accepted by the society. At 0.3 M level one is supposed to have enough knowledge of BOS. With further rise the knowledge and repeated observation his belief is strengthen leading to his awareness of BOS. At 0.5 M level his mind awakens with knowledge of IBC while realizing BOS. The effect of realization of BOS allows him to know the parameters of pleasure and differentiate sex as a short term pleasure thus trying to seek beyond. With grown up stage today it is known as material world. The material pleasure is similar and is off shoot on these lines. Possession of material is pleasure and there is no harm till it converts into greed and harming ones BOS and IBC and thus MS. Most of the human could easily drift towards the easier path and thus delay their growth.

why so?

The answer we would get in the next chapter.

But there would be few who do not drift and follow the tougher path which is leading to the higher mental level. As the natural crafted design by the creator the earlier reaching people are the one who have found solace and peace and do not bother for promoting the serenity they get. But down in the line and with time someone would come to propagate and who is recognized and would be trusted to follow the mind shift. The unending satisfaction is a typical mental feeling and best could be felt rather than explained. Because it can not be explained imparting the knowledge in the people who are busy in satisfying in material becomes difficult.

We have said earlier that till 0.5 M level human is influenced by the brain band and so the sex which has enabled to evolve in so many ways still find attraction for its physical portion for pleasure rather than for its purpose. One's pleasure also could convert into other's nightmare by those who do not want to rise. Crossing 0.5 M level the influence starts changing towards the other end of the band (that is I band which is not clearly visible and known till the moment). One word sex has all the ingredients overlapped and thus has the ability to make him realize about BOS. The first step forward in such situation is that he starts having knowledge of the mind (active mind as we would know further). The faint knowledge of the mind makes him explore more for IBC and makes him understand about the unending pleasure differentiating from a short term pleasure. The sex act clearly has the ability to bring the role of mind between the body and the pleasure and go further in the knowledge for the quest of self.

Different States of Mind

The Mental Synthesis (MS) which is generated in human has been the reason for rising in the process of our evolution but all would not take the best benefit due to the nature one has developed and utilization of their mental synthesis could be one reason.

Mental synthesis in a fear or the natural way

The mental level of a person indicates its specific location in the path of evolution between M=0 and M=1 at that point of time which is associated with a specific requirement of basic need and living habit. This level has the tendency to rise and with slightest rise ahead the requirement start changing for the body and mind to readjust or we can say that coordination among BOS, IBC and MS needs alteration and readjustments for a healthy and satisfied living.

It should be understood that in the process of living, every person takes a decision at every moment which is having a bearing in the formation of his habit. Bigger critical decisions are understood but there are small ones equally important which go unnoticed with the majority and become their bindings. The possible rise of mental level in one's lifetime could be as small as 0.03 M to 0.035 M but it could be significant if it is in one's knowledge as that would enable him to guide someone else to go forward in his knowledge.

How does one rise and how do one change habit?

There are distinctly two methods, people followed and the decision taken for small or big pertaining to onself could be as,

i. Feared state of mind or

ii. Natural flowing state.

Feared state

The test of a person in the rising mental level is critical when decision has to be taken. The probability of knowledge for such state also is in the same time. There is a conflict within him between what he wants and what he thinks he should have. The confusion is actually in what he thinks and what his mind thinks but the poor person is unable to distinguish and is forced for the decision and the action accordingly. Results could be satisfactory or otherwise. He could be pressurizing his mind without his knowledge or could be pressurizing himself without the knowledge of his mind.

Natural flowing state

In such state he does not think without the knowledge of his mind. For a step upward he tries to acquire knowledge of his BOS, IBC and MS and tries to readjust the proportion of load. The action and consequence by this method could be satisfactory or otherwise momentary. Those who follow such path do not get (or show as) upset on the immediate results. People develop habits such as sense of sacrifice, patience and tolerance. They would reduce the urge of comparison and expectation and could follow or improve on the discipline in their life.

Deeper and deeper knowledge of body organs and senses and gradual realization in steps has potential to generate all the basic references for whatever a human is searching continuously. External organs are understood very easily by anyone because they are physically seen and used but the total mechanism of working is far from one's limited (physical) knowledge. The senses are natural trait in all the species and have a significant role to play in human.

Let us consider what a 'Feeling' is.

It does not require action of any physical (external) organ. It is a mind which behaves as an organ for the action of the feeling. The action of a mind as an organ could be understood by an example of a child of 9 to 10 months.

If a child is shown a tree, fan or any other thing by his parent by pointing out his finger towards the object it may not register in the child's mind so early whereas if a cool breeze is blowing and if the child is explained about the feeling of cool breeze that would be understood much earlier.

It is irony that a pure and innocent mind of a child who does not possess the man-made communication is able to understand better about the thing (or feeling) invisible whereas with growing knowledge the understanding of physical picture makes understanding better than earlier. The reason is that the child is able to work with his mind clearly before he understands more in this world and gets confused.

Feared state or natural state is a behavior which one could inherit from very beginning or could try at any stage. The basic ingredient is available in all living and we human have the opportunity to tap the resource. The confusing state on the 'feeling' element can be observed in the following example,

M=0 is the closest state separating from the natural living where one is not be able to exploit the resources but has different strength for his survival provided by the superpower. Say for example animals adopt their living in different atmospheric conditions of extreme cold and warm where one would not have direct control in their way and they adjust their body conditions to bear the situation. They survive except for few of them whose destiny is over and if fate has to snatch few of them it would happen in any mental level and has to be accepted as the superiority of the creator. With growing in mental level and rising from M=0 human has become more intelligent and has brought variation in his thinking which is still half baked knowledge. For instance, using the same example of outside environmental condition of cold and hot weather he develops a fear to withstand the varying conditions. The element of mind which is governing the internal system (IBC) reduces the element to combat the cold weather in the feared state automatically. The MS works on the easier option for the control of weather by developing synthetic temperature controls in clothing or house by the so called comforts we know.

This does not intent to mean one should not protect oneself, not wear proper clothings or use air-conditioners etc. The majority of the people lie in such a bracket where they do require minimum of weather protection. Infact what has been allowed is a habit of body and mind in the general and in doing so we have underscored the power of mind within which lies infinite capability for combating for each smallest and biggest hurdle we could come across any time.

Realisation of Body Organs and Senses

In the mental level graph from M=0 to M=1 the intermediate point of 0.5 M level is of greater significance. As described earlier below this level a human is greatly influenced in his action and decision by the lower B band whereas beyond this point the influence starts switching over to the band ahead of M band. There are not many people who have reached today at this point for uplifting the society. Individually there are people at 0.5 M point and even higher but their being could be merely own effort to understand the creator. Their knowledge would not help the mass probably as the mass or the recognized leaders are not ready for that which could be a design of GOD.

Referring the example of cold and hot weather and protecting the body from the variation it is at 0.5 M level when one puts himself in doubt for the weakening ability to sustain the changed conditions. It is not only the changed weather that bothers but also all the decisions making requires a rethinking. One has reached at this stage due to the effort it would require the analysis of the efforts made in the knowledge or due to the circumstances or both and this process would lead to a better satisfying end. Even in the absence of whole knowledge one could develop the skill to understand the mind.

The basic concept remains the same as given for S equation. Deriving day-to-day satisfaction by adjusting the physical and mental effort which is a short term result oriented equation. If a person tries to adjust in few weeks he could know that either of his physical or mental effort was being underutilised or overutilised. Person at or near this level also would know that they have been switching the habits for whatever reason and thus possess much flexibility irrespective of the age one belongs. It is the understanding of his own body and it is for his well-being.

It does mean to have the ability of gathering knowledge, utilize each small decision for gaining the strength from the nearest level and such a person would not hesitate to gather the positive points from outside source as well. Difficult task is not so difficult if practiced earliest because whatever one knows is easy and to know, one has to practice. It is one lifetime, one gets to understand, realize and utilize the body and the mind. One utilises or loses the opportunity to make him more humane with a common destiny. A child is born and starts from a specific mental level due to his own past *karmas* (which would relate to the place , family and society where one is born) but at any level one is situated (be 0.2 M, 0.3 M, 0.4 M). The starting placement should not deter for going higher up and so should not have any regret because that would only help in delaying the process to understand oneself.

For the people at this stage there is no option other than to go up and rising 0.5 M level calls for the knowledge of body organ and senses. He already realizes pleasure and satisfaction. It is that further deeper knowledge of his organs and senses and their behavior would gradually unfold the mysteries to know about his own mind.

The Mind Power

Each part of the body has a very positive role to perform and external body and organs have much more capability than understood till now. Realization of body organs and senses above 0.5 M level could give the opportunity to have knowledge on this area. Realizing the roll of each body and organ part enables to improve the knowledge of mind. In fact in a lifetime whatever one thinks and does for his comfort or to acquire pleasure is for his body organ and senses which is half knowledge and most of the time it misleads the person.

Most of the time he thinks for protection, security and then luxuries and comforts in that order. The search continues and as destiny would tell some get in plenty and some get none. If he achieves all the best comforts he only gets the opportunity to strengthen his believe and thus moves ahead towards realization "that his knowledge for security and comfort for the body was a myth or a dream". It would not satisfy him and the situation would only force him to understand his mind which itself has the strength to fulfill the starting need in a better satisfying method.

If a person is bothered for the prime basic need, he would get from wherever destined without any problem *if* he is ready to work constructively in all situations and circumstances.

If he is thinking for security he would only know what would make him secure? Or what would actually help him to protect his body? If he thinks four wall enclosure could make him feel secure and is able to build such enclosure it would make one realise that he is still not secure and would generate the quest that he is in the search of something else.

The mental level of 0.7 M stated in the graph as shown in fig. 2.7 is the place which would give much higher knowledge of mind. There are people who have reached this place in the later stage of life to share their knowledge but would be short to establish the belief on others. The state would be self- satisfying to them where they might not be in a position to apply logics for the cause and effect for the larger society. What has to be understood that such situation also would come in centuries of years ahead that these would be basic things understood by everyone.

Coming back to the problem of security and four walls he would understand and redefine the meaning and would find that all the while he was in search of mental security and not for the body alone. Also he would know that not the four walls but the positive and the constructive work could only provide such security. He might understand and also know that he has wasted his non-returnable lifetime and can not blame anyone else for it.

It is YOU who possess a mind and so YOU think to possess the comforts and luxuries not because of fun but for the efficient utilization of your body. Your thought in this regard would be true to some extent but such adaptability could be surely underestimating the strength of mind. It has no other option than to make you synthetic. Delayed realization could only cause anxiety to find the mental rise very low and a wasteful life experience but what one is able to realise is due to his *karmas* in the earlier and even in this life and thus should be grateful to God and himself.

Knowledge of Mind

What would one gain by the knowledge of mind? The mind as we understand by time now is a section of our body constituent which makes human. In the next chapter we would understand that within the mind there are subdivisions causing anxieties and solution which we rarely try to probe. Referring to the knowledge of body organ and senses which is vital for knowing oneself is possible if mind exists. The knowledge of BOS which is gained at 0.3 M level starts turning into realization at 0.7 M level and this is the point where one starts having the knowledge of mind. Then the real positive utilization of the body starts appearing.

In a simpler term let us consider certain external body

organs and their parts and understand what they can do for our benefit.

Let us take an example of *hands*.

What can your hands do?

i. It can pluck fruits from a tree or vegetables out of a plant.

ii. It can assist to fulfill the basic needs in eating process.

iii. It can throw stones on others.

iv. It can try to defend the body on attack.

v. It can help in expressing your message.

vi. It can help in teasing another person.

vii. It can help feeling the joy and it can add pleasure to you.

Summing it up the hands could assist the body for its upkeep, defend and could also assist in destructive activity.

- In doing so the hand can make the mental orientation symmetric (could be momentarily) and
- The same hand could make the mental orientation asymmetric.

It is at an elevated level stage of mental level (0.7 M) one can know that the same hands in the subject could attempt in elevating mental levels of others.

Elevation of mental level should not be interpreted as a place where one could do magic and wonders. (It is true many who have reached in the understanding of wonders and have exploited it for their selfish end have been deprived of the wonders ahead in their reach). The elevated level starts unfolding the power of mind using the BOS and even IBC (at a later stage) as a tool for the work one could do beyond ones knowledge and is a natural art which calls for the purity of the mind. A person in such state his awareness or without knowing would have generic behavior following a discipline. Selfless life would have devotional attitude for a positive human cause.

Many might be not convinced with this for a simple reason explained earlier that before and after 0.5 M level one starts getting influenced by the character of brain and intellect bands. Existing before and after 0.5 M mental level and due to the influence the basic logics start changing.

A person below 0.5 M level who could have logic in his understanding and could develop a fight for his argument and this could appear a very insignificant for a person above 0.5 M level and could have the understanding of the ignorance of the former person. The knowledge of the basic organs internal and external could be first stage of knowing not only of our body-mind but the universe as well. There is so much to know within the closest available things to enlighten us beyond the imagination of an ordinary man.

Let us go in deep for some more external body organs indicating the power of mind.

We took the example of hand. Going further fingers and nails are two components the hand would possess and let us see if these components have some strength to indicate mind power.

- *Fingers* help to hold the food to eat.
- *Fingers* also assist to balance the body in the process of standing or sitting while changing the posture.

These arts are carried out naturally without the knowledge of his mind.

Similarly, *Fingers* with mental application could run over the body and coordinate with different locations to reduce or remove physical body disorders of pains and cramps. We read about acupressure and other science for reducing physical disorders which has come out from such knowledge. We know such therapy does not work equally on all. Irrespective of any such knowledge of science what we are saying here is that those small fingers you have are capable of far more utility for yourself at the first moment before it serves any good to others.

But can anybody do it?

Yes.

Only if one could try to feel the mind by the help of the fingers he could definitely do it.

But how do you know which mental level you belong to or if the mental orientation is symmetric as an essential component.

Let us take the same hand and the finger and test them.

- Place the fingers of right hand on the left palm.
- Gently tap the fingers on the palm.
- Now reverse the finger and the palm so that finger selected is of left hand and tapping is done on the right palm.
- Do this concentrating on the action. Do this while chatting with others.
- Do this with open eyes looking at the action. Do this with closed eyes.

This simple action could have different results to different persons at different mental levels and mental orientations at that moment.

A person around 0.3 M level in all the above situation would be simply able to see as a physical act. Around 0.5 M level the act with closed eyes could generate a different feeling which subsequently could be felt even with open eyes.

The special feeling of tapping could highlight the knowledge of the mind. What does it mean?

i. The mind is continuously interacting with BOS, IBC and MS as described earlier but the person himself is not aware of in most of the time.

ii. The IBC is not physically seen and is difficult for an ordinary person to visualize.

iii. The knowledge of mind as tapping of finger in such instance in a symmetric higher mental level condition is even able to correlate with IBC.

iv. Result is that those fingers are further able to map the body and locate a point to correct IBC for any discomfort feeling.

Our next example is of *Nails* of the fingers.

The *Nails* are essentially a dead material in itself and a useful waste produced by the body. Nails could be having the utility in the Stone Age if at all. Its deadness can be understood as there is no pain in cutting it.

Do we know that the mind is the source for all the actions internal and external for all the three core areas of BOS, IBC and MS with or without our knowledge?

This means that mind has to labour with the internal process (IBC) to segregate the nail forming material from the received intake and make it reach to the proper place.

The nails could make fingers look better and could be helpful as a protecting cover but at the cost of the burden on mind for completing its process which if reduced could give benefit to a person in something more useful. A real significance may not be visualized today but when bulk of people would reach level around 0.7 M the utility would be strongly emerge in redefining the food habits so that the load on the mind is reduced on this exercise and is used elsewhere.

Let us take another example of *Hair*.

The *hair* is once again a dead material generated by the body. It is not an organ, has no sense but the body has to grow and the mind has to labour. The hairs grow grey with age.

The hairs also grow grey with stress and strain as we know.

If we assume 60 or 70 years as a natural ageing period of a person, grey hair at that point of time could be considered as a natural factor but if stress causes hairs to grey at 40 or 50 years or even before what should be considered?

Focusing this phenomena with our discussion if mind and its functional duties we would see that,

i. The graying of hair has relation with internal chemistry (IBC).

ii. IBC is controlled by mind.

iii. Person having stress and strain would mean putting extra load on the mind.

iv. The mind is laboring for BOS, IBC and MS in its best capacity.

v. Overstraining would cause imbalance somewhere and affect could be visible in any or all the three components.

Graying of hairs is one such visible thing to attract attention.

There could be other symptoms felt by the individual simultaneously relating IBC for physical disorder, obesity or any other issue to make him bothered.

The symptom of early hairs graying would indicate early aging and it would mean stagnation of mental level.

And further it could imply that the basic equation of S=1 is highly imbalanced and the result would be discontentment.

How would a person at elevated mental level behave and control such situation?

His understanding of BOS and IBC being higher would be able to try and orient his mental frame in symmetric fashion. He would be able to exercise necessary controls required for that and would be able to prevent any undue load on the mind.

His hair would not only grey in its proper time but when they grey as a natural state that would add grace on him as well. If a proper oriented (symmetric) mind could understand the quality and the quantity of the food intake and if he follows it, the mind would not tend to exhaust in the formation of useless waste thus producing a thin growth.

Few examples are sited here for hands, fingers and hairs. The cause and effect for each small organ external as well as internal and the parts of the body relating to those organs would have a significant role to play. The mind is there to control each of them along with additional duty of mental synthesis (MS). It has the capability for maneuvering meticulously only if we allow working as it wants.

The mind therefore is much more than we understand. Let us know the basics of mind in more details in the next chapter.

3

Mind and Anti-Mind

We have discussed the ascending ladder of mental level. We have indicated that a human is born at a specific mental level and his lifetime goes up in the ladder. The growth in a lifetime of an enlightened person is also quite small going by the fig.3.0. The enlightened leaders are the one who understand the body-mind system better and assist others to lift in their mental level. These persons have positive energy and use their mind in positive way and thus actions of BOS, IBC and MS are positive. Inspite of this fact the average folk does not follow the same way because all have their own mind and thus their own interpretation towards the life. The essay has been focusing the positive aspect or the portion of such leaders who have helped and are helping to evolve with time.

We have described the duties of mind that it has to perform in its knowledge or ignorance.

We have discussed about the mental orientation and its nature of being symmetric or asymmetric. This nature could be momentary or changing one but does have the implication in cultivating a habit and thus the overall nature of himself. If the nature of one remains asymmetric most of the time or very often and he is unable to understand or improve upon, character thus he would develop out of it would be very different to a person who is able to keep or reorient in symmetric type easily. If mind has given the knowledge of pleasure and satisfaction the majority are in the grip of the knowledge of displeasure and frustration creating disharmony and turbulence in their life.

What is this mind?

The mind is not a mystery for an intelligent human. Apart from all the activities it does, the mind is a tool of intelligent human to know far more than the body organ senses. And to go further ahead one has to apply his mind and understand it. We human are good in understanding things in a physical form better and thus the diagram as in fig. 3.0 as a mind would be easy to explain.

The figure shows a small circle as 1 encircled by another circle 2 in a bigger circle 3.

The bigger circle 3 is shown as the area to which a mind can expand mentioned as 1.0 M. (which would be equal to the mental level M=1 where we evolving human have yet to reach).

The two circles 1 and 2 are the real ones that are being used by a human and rest space to expand is an open space available.

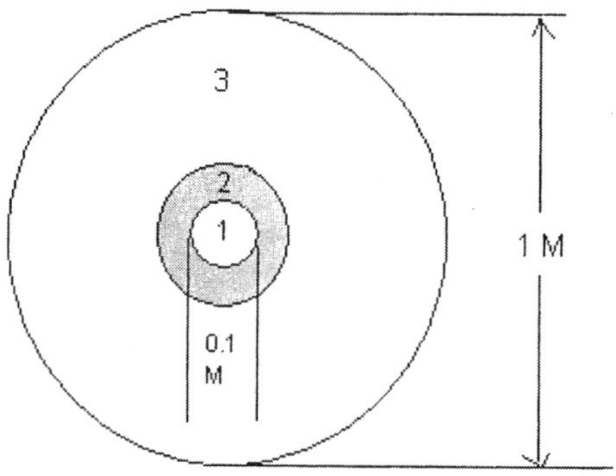

Fig. 3.0

Circle 1 shown in this specific case as 0.1 M indicates a human with mental level of 0.1 M.

Positive and Negative Element

Mental synthesis (MS) has been the cause in human making and the moment he has acquired a bit he has left the natural path adopted by animals. The mental synthesis has given the primary basic knowledge of love to understand the new life further. Further down what he has observed is that either he has got enough of love or has been deprived of it. In the process of evolution further he has acquired the knowledge of respect where again he has either observed to live in harmony where respect prevailed in their society and also observed the jealousy and guilt where there has been scarcity of respect in their society. Further in the path he had developed the knowledge of ego and developed pride to cause problem within.

The human traits thus described emerged in the process of evolution are of positive and negative in nature. These are directly not derived from anybody – organ or senses though their role are utilised in the process for communication. It is the additional charge which person is handling and is liable to create more complication and confusion in absence of proper understanding. These elements prevail in all the possible mental levels and with mental level rising it would lead to either more complicated situation or a better understanding. This nature has to exist in the MIND band irrespective one has knowledge about it or not and is reflected in the nature of a person. Once a person has slightest knowledge these elements surface out and there is a struggle between the mind and himself. Once he realizes its importance or starts understanding his mind, he tends to move up in the mental level. In the other probability, if he does not obey his mind he tends to confuse and only is able to distort the symmetric mental orientation which could lead to a negative atmosphere around him.

Every and any action done by the body or any thought coming in a human has a positive or negative aspect. If mind is operating three elements viz. BOS, IBC and MS negative act of one has unknowingly impact on others in a negative manner.

But what is negative?
Is anything good or bad?

Anything good for me could be bad for you or vise-versa.

It requires better interpretation.

I consume alcohol, I think I like it and enjoy it but in fact I donot try to see the impact on the mind and consequently the effect is seen in all my own world of BOS, IBC and MS.

Beating, abusing, killing and many such acts are negative which could be easily understood by a very layman and similarly each and every organ and senses have a negative way to act. It could be a matter of dispute to many to accept even a small thing as negative because they do it but whatever further they do is only try to defend their act and can be successful in a physical sense. For such instance, if we leave the argument and the justification the person at least knows he has committed an act which has resulted in generating a story which relates to MS. Similarly, there would be positive and negative impact due to various reasons side effecting IBC (internal body chemistry) going unnoticed to him.

- One's body may require a salted food and he consumes more of sweet because he thinks he likes it and is enjoying it.
- One's body may require one bowl of food but consumes two bowls full as it is appearing palatable to the tongue.

If consuming alcohol is negative, consuming wrong amount or selecting the wrong food for the body is equally negative.

At the mental synthesis level, if you laugh you also cry, if you have ego, you also insult. You love and also hate and so there distinctively can categorize positive and negative features. Thus in all the three spheres of BOS, IBC and MS there is a negative or positive action taking place and indirectly action of one has its effect on others as well. Further we also have seen that there could be any of the following probabilities,

i. I am aware of the mind and try to overrule it for any action or

ii. I have no knowledge about the mind v/s the action taken.

Any person would be experiencing both of the states in different context and different state of his knowledge and would be responsible in making his nature accordingly.

Here it is important to know that the **MIND never works negative** and its sole purpose is to interact with all the three areas of BOS, IBC and MS in a positive way.

If the mind is working in positive direction what is contributing the negative element?

It is **anti-mind*** within a person which prompts for negative action.

From where does the anti-mind come?

**Anti-mind is the word coined here for a useful description of the subject. The word mind has been used in its general meaning but here onwards we would be using two separate word mind and anti-mind according to the impact they generate.*

In fact the moment mind has come in picture over brain the anti-mind is associated and with the advancement we could be in a state to have a better knowledge about it. Anti-mind is married with the mind and thus existed from the very moment mind has come in picture but if its location and duty is understood properly that could differentiate the role.

Anti-mind: As soon as a mind is formed there is a thin layer of anti-mind over it.

The thin anti-mind layer resists the growth of mind. The outlook for anything varies with the degree of anti-mind layer existing.

Anti-mind has a significant role in the entire system of human and so becomes important to understand in depth and knows the difference with that of the mind.

Let us refer Fig.3.0 once again,

i. Small clear circle marked as 1 is the area occupied by the mind.
ii. Shaded area around 1 marked as 2 is occupied by anti-mind and
iii. The entire area 3 in the section is the upper limit in which mind or anti-mind has to grow with evolution.

1 M marked is the ultimate growth of mind. The entire area could be occupied by mind and anti-mind with different proportions generating different behavior. Till the present evolution we have not reached a state to occupy the complete circle be with mind or anti-mind. If few persons would have reached they are not in the knowledge of the world and so in the scientific and informative world we could assume that none have reached there.

We have explained about the existence of the brain in animal world and also said that in this band one lives in the boundary of minimum skills for the survival. The human state applies when mind comes in the picture within the brain which has made our evolution dynamic in a non-returnable path.

Let us consider again the Fig.3.0, which shows a primary level of mind when it has grown to the mental level equal to 0.1 M. We also know now that 0.1 M mental level,

i. Would have a meaning for the requirement of a definite amount of physical and mental labour for satisfaction.
ii. It would also imply a person to have a specific food habit along with utilization of certain mental synthesis.

As in brain segment the circular loops were there naturally to perform the related group in natural instinct in this platform and in the above example 0.1 M mind there is naturally a tiny layer of anti-mind formed. In another term over a positive mind controller there is a thin layer of anti-mind which is negative in nature and has a tendency to question oneself with questions of IFS and WHYS. The area

3 marked in the figure is the expansion space that the mind and anti-mind together can grow to the maximum.

The creator, the God is so supreme not only in powers but also in the craftsmanship that he has not made a slightest flaw in his work. If in the brain band animals live in the natural circuit to maintain the equilibrium in the natural system, it is one positive (mind) and one negative (anti-mind) feature brought in the mind segment again to keep the system in equilibrium.

Realization of the positive and negative elements also emerges from the natural instincts and behavior and from body organ and senses. Requirement of food is positive and that is why quality and quantity of food change is required with different mental levels for a stable (satisfied) situation. Food for body tends to give food for thought and assists for food for mind to rise. Whereas sex is the natural negative element gifted to a human. It operates not by the mind *but only by anti-mind* which should be understood very nicely.

Anti-Mind the Hurdle in the Growth of Mind

From the time mind has emerged in a human to the slightest extent (say 0.1 M) marked as 1 in the fig. 3.1A there has been two probabilities to move ahead at a position 2 A or 2 B. It is important to understand from the figure that,

i. In 1 which is representing 0.1 M mental level total active part is equal to x amount.
ii. Whereas in 2 A and 2 B the total active part is equal to y within the outer periphery of inner circle drawn. The total active area y is increased than fig. 3.1 A part 1.
iii. Accordingly between 2 A and 2 B the total active area are equal but the clean and shaded areas are different which show two different active ingredients forming a nature of a person.
iv. The clear area beyond the x or y portions but within the main circle is the one that could be expanded. This expansion would happen with time and with generations of evolution.

In figure 1 x portion includes two sections,

i. Clear portion working as mind and

ii. Shaded portion working as anti-mind.

The mind comes with a thin layer over it in a natural state. The thin layer is of anti-mind. By gradual elimination of anti-mind, layer one could rise and reach the higher level stated as 0.3 M shown as 2 B in the figure.

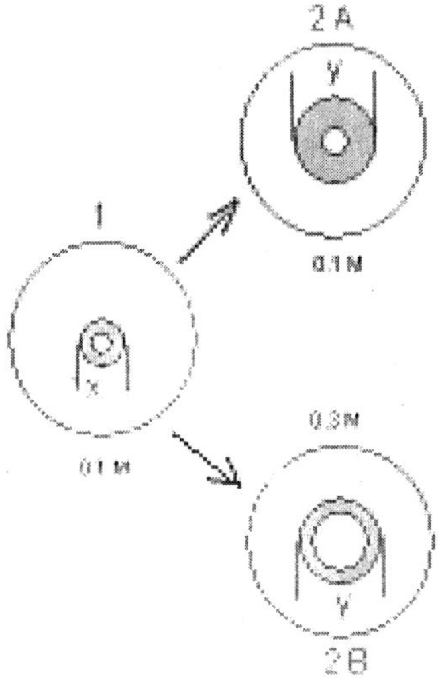

Fig. 3.1 A

There is another possibility that occurs in people where he is not ready to understand about the thin layer and not ready to force his mind for different activities he is doing day to day. Such person could make his active area reach at 2 A of the figure. The status of 2 A and 2 B are mirror image with both having same active area but one with 0.3 M mind and an anti-mind while the other is barely 0.2 M and rest filled with anti-mind. Anti-mind is a negative portion and in climbing a small step 2 A person has thickened the negative portion.

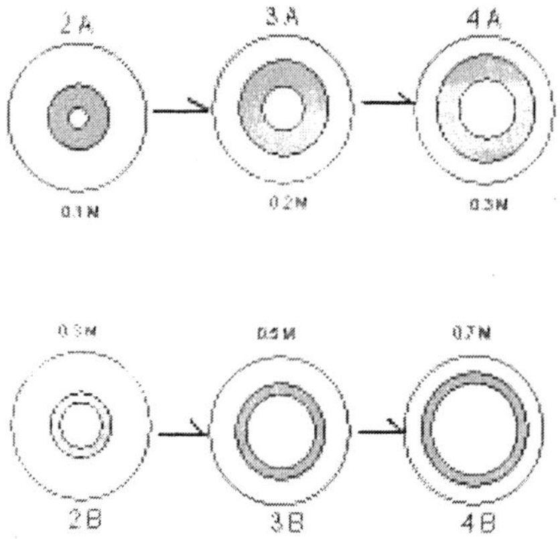

Fig. 3.1 B

We have considered 2, 3 and 4 as significant stages in the mental evolution of a self of which we would be discussing further. In each stage of progress from point 1 one would be moving ahead in the direction of 2 then 3 and then towards 4 A person situated at 4 B has lifted his mental level to 0.7 M (which is significantly quite high and not many have reached this place yet) but the corresponding 4A person who has risen very less (0.3 M) has thickened the anti-mind to such an extent that he would require tremendous force to crack and thus would only ensure *not to have mental piece and would have negative behavior for any and every part of his body, mind interaction.* In such event it is possible that a person at 4 A starts interpreting the mind element as anti-mind.

If life is a dream the outlook towards the dream is entirely different visualized by one at 4 A level to that one at 4 B. If two persons in 4 A and 4 B conditions are standing side by side, 4 A conditioned person would think him to be equal and would like to equate or imitate to the other at 4 B whereas the other one belongs to much higher mental level with different needs and habitat at equilibrium state. The result is that 4 A conditioned person would try to physically impress that he is superior whereas actually his stable and equilibrium state would require more of physical activity and less of mental labour. Here if he tries to think and say he is superior he is neglecting his own mind which is making the effort to state him and realize about his actual condition.

Contrary a person in 4 B condition would not think that he is superior but would only try to gain more knowledge and share some with others.

Landmarks in the Path of Changing Mental Level

In the above example we have cited stage 1, 2, 3 and 4. These stages have importance of different landmarks in the process of movement. Though there would be definite steps before one reaches from point 1 to 2 and then to 3 and then to 4, and even a small rise from 1 to 2 could take many ages or generation each of these points have specific feature which are highlighted in self. The features highlighted in self relate to mind and anti-mind which surface out as the nature of an individual.

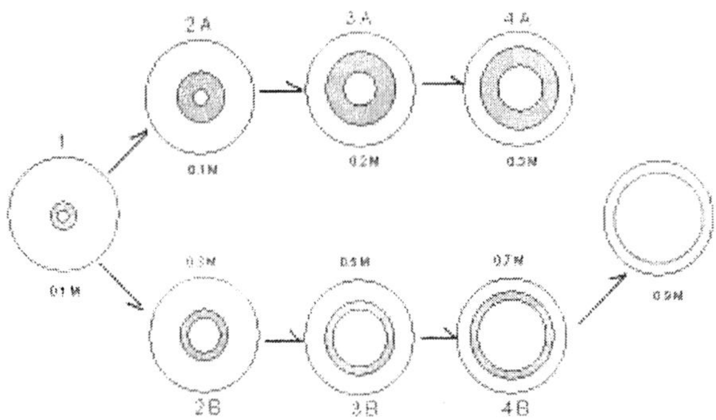

Fig. 3.2

We have seen that there are three elements of BOS, IBC and MS on the physical level that work in tandem in a self and three elements of knowledge, awareness and skill would do all work together in making oneself realized to the highest level that is 1.0 M where no one has yet reached. Let us see in steps how we rise in steps. For our discussion we have generally considered three landmark levels mentioned but there would be many sub steps between the two which is not highlighted.

Point 1 is the starting factor so we reach the point 2.

2 B: 0.3 M Factor

With mind entering the brain (it makes human) the changes start taking place in the living being. Once he has the knowledge of mental application (MS) the slight knowledge of anti-mind could surface out or increase sharply if not observed in the behavior. The anti-mind which is always there as a thin layer tends to increase over the mind section and 0.3 M (2 B in the figure) is the first major crossing where the primary negative element is exposed in the form of comparison in a self. The primary parameter surfacing out is comparison in the MS. Both mind and anti-mind work on comparison on a very different way. If comparison could be used to lift oneself and others, same comparison could be used negatively for creating a thicker anti-mind.

How it happens?

If one would compare the strength, compare the beauty, compare the diet, compare the position one is actually comparing his anti-mind to that of his mind whereas the person thinks that he is comparing with another person or his trait. The element of comparison occupies the area MS in the mind (anti-mind) which is also tackling BOS and IBC at the same time. As this section is controlling all three elements simultaneously and in the absence of his own knowledge anti-mind could be utilizing this trait of comparison in the present case. In such a situation over utilization of MS by anti-mind would destabilize the other two portions of BOS and IBC which could be in his knowledge or without knowledge. This act would bring instability in self and would feel disgusted by his efforts and would be restricting the elevation of mind and hurting oneself.

Let us take an example.

I compare my small house with one of my friend's palatial building. Now be small house or a palace both are man-made non-living things that can never be the source for generating anxiety.

But what happens!

Even with closed eyes and sitting back on an old cot my anti-mind tries to see the beauty of the interior with the addition of desires to be with beautiful living beings. The anti-mind is trying to feel the coziness of sitting in the room, sleeping or working in the room and trying to feel the comfort of the air-conditioning. It is trying to taste the delicacies of known and unknown things. Here unknowing utilization of organs and senses has a significance and in this case it is a wasteful practice at the cost of self and nobody else.

The main struggle is between mind and anti-mind. Comparison is between organ senses (BOS) and the mental syntheses (MS) and what happens is that the internal body chemistry (IBC) goes unaware. Such a situation would generate improper composition and various operations inside happening would be affected resulting in disorder in the total system. It could lead to obesity, newer diseases, minor physical disorders, and minor mental disorders.

If in a situation one does not realizes it soon one is only thickening the anti-mind and making it more powerful and in such situation one is not only restricting the mental rise but also losing the time and the opportunity of the actual capability which could make one reach to the point of satisfaction and the contentment.

Let us see the same example but with another situation.

One makes a strong desire to achieve a palatial building and he is determined for it in any circumstance. It is said generally that a strong determination yields a positive results.

What happens now?

He is determined to empower his anti-mind and ready

to take the risk in the due course. With anti-mind in power and adopting risk taking attitude all sort of negative habits would surface out and the result could be,

- Either one would develop a thick anti-mind making far from having any mental peace he could tend to create a mental disorder, could lead to nervous break down or his organ and senses appear to fail by the time he achieves is desired material value or
- Could be that he has taken lesser risks and if he is not badly affected in the course of time there is a probability he had some realization which could have improved his mental level but anti-mind could not give the mental peace irrespective he achieves the material desire (a palatial building in this case).

There is yet another probability in the same example.

One desires for the palatial building and for that he develops the anti-mind but as luck would happen he gets the palace without any efforts as a gift from someone. Now with immediate achieving the results from unknown and unexpected quarter the questions that would be generated are,

- *Am I prepared for such a gift? or*
- *What next would be the expected query in the anti-mind?*

There is a probability that the realization could help to lift the mental level to readjust the anti-mind which would reflect in the attitude and this could be destiny of his own *karmas* not in his knowledge.

But if the *karmas* have been negative and one gets a palace making him overjoyed for the gift from unknown quarter the same question of

Am I prepared for such a gift and what next?

- Would create another web on the anti-mind to reach the next level of complexity of thinking oneself superior and adding never ending ego problems.

Should this mean one must not have any desire, not take any risk, not be determined!

In the first case if possible definitely yes but that is not the issue.

What one needs is to understand the anti-mind which in turn gives the opportunity to understand the mind for achieving the same results.

What would be different then?

The proper understanding and willingness to understand self would clarify that if the results are required of quantitative nature or qualitative nature.

The anti-mind is capable of giving quantitative and quick results except for his own *karmas* which can add quality as well. On the other hand the mind has capability to give the qualitative end irrespective one achieves the results soon or late or not at all. Here by "not at all" it should be understood that the time would have made him realized that the goal set was not good and so would allow to alter the goal by the mind beneficial for him. There are chances that this statement could not be accepted by the management persons of the economic world today but could be understood easily by a person undergone through such state.

Any decision taken by self in the management at home or the office could give desired result or not. If the risk (or the step) is taken to the extent one is ready to bear it easily, financially or emotionally it could be argued that it is not a risk and if the risk is taken beyond the bearable limit then the job of mind does come in picture. By the mind one could know the step would never be negative and would allow him or caution the movement which is conducive for the self and the larger cause. The destiny not being his ability to see he keeps obeying the mind and the result with reference to organ and senses (BOS), internal body chemistry (IBC) and mental synthesis (MS) he is able to take more risk and is more determined and is capable to win over his anti-mind and achieve the goal.

3 B: 0.5 M Factor

0.5 M factor is the second important ladder which one has reached due to his own effort. By the satisfaction equation derived earlier it is a state where one requires 50 % energy to be spent of physical nature and 50 % energy of mental nature. It is the time and his living which has taught him and made him bring at this point knowingly or unknowingly. 0.5 M state automatically infers that one has become quite aware about his organ and senses which would mean he has picked up the habit of listening to others even if he does not follow or agree. Some patience has been developed but it could be haunting him at time on the upsurge of anti-mind.

This state also signifies that one has increased knowledge about internal body chemistry which would mean that he has understanding of good and bad for his body requirement even though one may not be religiously following the rule. People could be obsessed by the information available today about the nutrition and could be trying to balance their diet which necessarily does not mean the knowledge of IBC. The knowledge of IBC varies for individuals according to their nature, brought up and their mental level.

If at 0.3 M level it was comparison and strong physical desire which were prone for building anti-mind one has overcome to a larger extent in either case if he has achieved or not. If you are at 0.5 m level you have won over the comparison but going up the ladder again you are enveloped by a new thin layer of superiority complex or ego problem. The desire was of physical nature and comparison was of man-made material and had an advantage of realization sooner and with ease irrespective one got it or not for the reason that one can directly see and feel it. The new landmark of 0.5 M level is deprived of this advantage and thinks "I am superior".

- I may be a king,
- I may be a breadwinner,
- I may be a mill owner,
- I may be a manager.

In any of such situation 'I' thinks that others should follow me, obey me, respect me and so on.

I am determined, I frame rules, ask to follow laid down laws but the other person breaks the rule. My anti-mind becomes active and feels insulted.

This is the stage of mental level where one has the capability to know positive and negative and could know if he is asking for positive or negative but his anti-mind is so strong that it only tries to be ignorant of mind by the very nature of anti-mind it only tries to exploit the situation and know that IGNORANCE IS BLISS but forgets that by closing eyes he is still visible to others. Similarly, the anti-mind only tries to be ignorant of mind which exactly has the idea of good and bad, positive and negative and the result is that he gets agitated over his mind. The superiority complex or the ego problem is of your anti-mind over your mind and nothing else which surfaces out in different physical forms.

In such a situation, if mind tries to open up the covered ignorance because of the very nature of the mind two probabilities could emerge,

(a) Either anti-mind is ready to accept to reduce this negative layer. This could be in small steps such that a little knowledge and its application leads to awareness and thus towards realization of its intent or

(b) Anti-mind is jealous about the activities of mind and when it knows that the mind cannot be kept ignorant and it tries to use the organ and senses to prove its point*. When this layer is thickened mind has not much option than to cool down.

* *It should be known that body organ and senses are the only tools with which the anti-mind can play whereas the mind has more to that.*

The actual struggle is of your anti-mind over your mind and what actually happens is that you fight with others with whom you are associated in different walks of the life. These other persons could be in service with you, could be your dependent in family, could be persons who simply respect you but your view is different. Your anti-mind is trying to create more layers over the mind.

The anti-mind does not know but is the source of your creation. It only knows its strength and thinks that it could create a mind where it fails. Anti-mind definitely can create a body; it can also create another anti-mind but can never create a mind which is guided from somewhere else.

Referring fig. 3.2 if one situated in 3 B position of 0.5 M level and if there is another person in front of him at 3 A level with a thicker anti-mind layer and actually of much lower mental level the difference of approach could be gauged for the similar requirements. If 3 A person insults 3 B because of his nature he has developed 3 B person would only pity him because of his knowledge of his state. 3 B would be patient, bear him and the affect of 3 B mind is in so powerful position that it would try to reduce the anti-mind of person in front of him (3 A in this case) in the process.

0.5 M level is state which could benefit others but at this point it does not know the real power which it could possess in elevating his own mental level along with others coming in influence to him.

3 B: 0.7 M Factor

Fig.3.2:4 B is the position of 0.7 M level whereas the mirror image is 4 A. There are plenty at 4 A position but very scanty in their active life at 4 B who could influence the society. This position would have greater importance with time to come as we can understand by its significance. If one has crossed over 0.5 M level it would mean that he is successful in scrapping the anti-mind layer to rise and gradually come across a new cross road of 0.7 M. This landmark is achieved by one's own effort and his *karmas* but to remember that a new anti-mind layer appears with much more complexity.

In your rising from 0.5 M to 0.7 M level you definitely have ego but lesser ego problems. Your mind has the knowledge and a diminished anti-mind layer. Now the new anti-mind layer developed allows you to think that "you have won". The mind never thought of it but at this stage the anti-mind says that you have won over others. It demands recognition, it demands power, it demands authority.

BUT TO WHOM?

Actually over his own mind.

The mind never reacts to violence, never reacts instantaneously as it knows that it does not have any positive significance and exactly the opposite the anti-mind reacts. This time the anti-mind reacts not to show its supremacy but to win, to get the power and it makes you to do the beastly acts or even worse.

Ironically only after the thought it has won it is now overreacting to win. If the new layer over the mind is not reduced anti-mind which has been trying all sorts of illusion over the mind is only on the verge of getting confused itself. Such state would confuse you and also confuse others in the influence. In the existing social system if you have any authority, if you have any powers actually your deeds have made reach this stage BUT simultaneously confuses many others again who are trapped because of their own *karmas*.

May be your deeds or misdeeds were not to the extent to give you the authorative position at this level and so the anti-mind layer does not stop to play its negative role. It demands recognition. This layer uses your organ senses as the tool for the unwanted risk with quantification and justification and may or may not get the results.

Lucky are those who do not get the results. Spontaneous decision, quantification, justification all are time orientated matter and if had the positive value the mind would have done it in a better way and not for the cause the ant-mind is doing if it can help in convincing others it is actually again getting confused over the mind and this state is so bad that it could tend to block the mental level elevation further till the body-organ-senses ceases to obey their function because of their excessive use (or abuse).

As many people in their active stage have not reached

this stage it could be well understood by the mirror image state of 4 A in the fig. 3.2. The anti-mind layer has grown so thick that it tries by all means to power the mind and for that reason it makes the body organ senses to behave in the fashion, "I am the most powerful", such person would shout, hit, kick, assault, victimize and so on. What is happening infact the anti-mind is avoiding something which you tend to see by mind. The method best adopted by anti-mind is over utilization of body-organ-senses and over-utilizing these elements itself deprives him for going up the ladder because of the time lapse of your lifespan. In case, if there is a realization then it would not be beneficial for others because if there is slightest realization the next move would be to interact with internal chemistry which must have been deteriorated in the process and which is equally important to bring oneself in equilibrium to rise.

The Glimpses of Power

Refreshing the subject we have seen that species in brain segment are creatures other than human being who live in a natural circuit keeping the system and surrounding in harmony.

We have seen that mind element had emerged in the brain making a different species of human as we know who has worked for breaking the natural law of harmony in the system. Mind and anti-mind have been the positive and negative elements of this segment which have resulted in creating a maze of human being in different mental levels performing different acts without knowing the effective consequence in the mankind and their role in such act. Human have developed values and thus a society that could enable to live in harmony but that does not mean all is well. One rule can not support the requirement of people with varying mental levels. Human have done technical adventures and for that reason too much of materialism has been generated irrespective one actually requires it or not.

The persons who have risen in mental level have not been influenced by such things and for that reason there could be not many but rise of few such people against the odds have been entirely due to their effort to win over themselves and could be the effect of their own *karmas* of yester lives. In this life they have experienced their world from a different angle. Even when they have acquired a good amount of knowledge they feel that there is so much to learn. If they are different from the mass they have done something remarkable which they do not know or they would have not done something what all others would tend to do.

It is important to add the knowledge to the readers that 1.0 M stage which we would not be discussing is not the last stage of human development but is only the last segment of mind segment beyond which additional segment emerges from it as Intellect band. Intellect band 'I' starts from the point the mind segment reaches its peak of 1.0 M.

The mental level of 0.7 M is the stage represented as 4 B in the fig. 3.2 would be the biggest milestone of the present mankind. It is not that persons are not existing in this stage but they either do not have enough knowledge about it or are not recognized on the day. Such people would have tendency for the selfless service and they would be doing in the human community and not focused on issues of name or fame which is the demand of such state. It is the scientific power, material power which is over shadowing the growth of such people to come in the limelight and would continue till someone reaches 1.0 M level. The lot who are coming closer to 1.0 M in absence of the knowledge and their strength are influenced of 'I' level and so have the different outlook.

If such people have gone far ahead in the mental level what is that they see different?

and what could they provide others in this material world which they are also a part of it?

We would explore these probabilities.

Awareness of BOS

A person at the crucial mental stage himself may not know about the powers he is acquiring and the smallest gain unknowingly is not wasted even if he has not known and utilized. As soon as he moves slightest fraction ahead of 0.7 M level he starts coming in the influence of another superior band and his approach for everything starts altering.

The mind band has been woven with BOS, IBC and MS and so let us sees the difference from this base itself. Before reaching to this level one knows the strength of your body organ and senses because he has been utilizing them effectively. For instance,

- One knows the strength of his eyes. He does not stare at any living being but tries to use it delicately (or miserly) or
- One could appear to be gazing constantly at some object (as observed by another person) but actually could be seeing far beyond the reach with naked eyes.

Such state itself calls for having capability to understand good or bad and reaching to this level would mean better control over his mind and anti-mind. In such a state if any bad moment comes through one's life one would not close his eyes but would try to bother his mind to the minimum level and thus not allow much interaction between anti-mind and the BOS, IBC and MS that could generate unnecessary anxieties.

When interacting with a group in such a state you could be looking at all of them or none of them. If you happen to guide someone on a correct path and see him eye to eye the realization of strength appears when the other person is never in a position for argument or contradict the lesson. Eye is one such organ with its multi-functional capabilities written down.

Each of the external and internal organ and senses have been operated through mind or anti-mind or no mind with different impact on the self. At higher mental level one has acquired capability to utilize many of the organs through the mind. Each small insignificant part of the body has a role to play for self-realization and it comes only by proper utilizing it. External organs which could give the direct impact physically can be noticed and understood easily. Let us take another organ mouth for our study.

Among BOS, IBC and MS the first element remain as a tool as before but its usage and implication on other viz. IBC and MS make all the differences. Further realization of BOS would mean that one is able to link its impact with rest of the two elements. For a person of this level the second element IBC also would be better understood and the process of learning is to link with MS with more clarity. Let's take mouth as an example of an organ which could be more easily linked with MS. Mouth used for talking can be interpreted as a direct link with MS. We know the primary function of mouth for eating for any kind of species but in human the significance is higher. Talking or sharing the thoughts to each other has been the root cause for human evolution. Talking or expressing the views have surfaced positive and negative elements. If comparison has been said as one negative element in the earlier part of the mental rise it remains a mystery for a person in a lower mental level but for you at 0.7 M level it is very clear. When you talk to another person of lower mental level you would know the limitations of that person and so try to find out the positive element in him for lifting him from his base level. You may use same negative 'comparison' as tool to upgrade him.

- You know every person has some positive strength irrespective of any situation and levels. You would highlight the strength with the similar negative value suitable for his level as 'comparison' in this case with the strengths in others to make one feel happy feel elevated about. Utilization of such technique is done only if it helps to realise and uplift him and never for exploitation which he has been using in his state.

Such elevated state would know that hands which can patiently carve huge statues is a better way of constructive activity rather than only selling them.

The new reached mental stage itself infers that one has realization of organ and senses to a larger extent. Realization is a state where one would not intend to hurt any other living being in his knowledge. In fact all the organs and senses now act only when they see *through the mind.* This is the stage when he is getting closer to the intellect band and so one starts getting the knowledge that his various organs and senses are controlled by the mind and so his new interest is generated in further experiencing to utilize the mind to control the organ and senses. The organs–sense have been the tool since beginning but operating them through the mind would mean to use them as necessary tools only. This further prompts him to utilize his tools efficiently. The realization of organ and senses as a tool of his mind enables him to think that any excessive use would generate disharmony within him and he would loose the new generated spirit which is the taste of power yet unknown to him. It is a very important state and the indication of his approaching the INTELLECT BAND.

His knowledge of fate is very different from the one in the lower mental level.

How?

He knows that he has reached at this stage only because of his minimally using negative elements of BOS, IBC and MS and thus acquired some power within him. He is also aware that for basic survival he has to overstrain some of his organ and senses which he would do at the cost of his own power attained and that would be his fate.

Knowledge of IBC

At this stage one has reached the stage of realization for most of the organ and senses but as he has still many elements remaining to master could be called in awareness state. Similarly in the IBC region quite awareness has been achieved in the totality of the body system but in absence for complete awareness his knowledge certainly has grown substantially.

What that means?

It is the knowledge of internal body chemistry. It is all about the internal organ functioning its requirement and method to strain those parts to the minimum. Food which is essential for survival is important in the knowledge. Selection of food may be not directly in his own hands but in this advanced state his mind knows the actual body requirement both quantity wise and quality wise. Qualitatively and ideally 0.7 M state would require easily digestible food in very less quantity which would vary from person to person for him to judge and with the associated activities one is doing. This type of food would give the taste and simultaneously exert less labour to the organ in processing and thus putting lesser labour on their mind for the IBC reaction.

The availability of such food or the quality could be out of his bound for various reasons and in such situation the capability in him exists in readjusting his system in one of the following ways,

a. Either the mind maneuvers the basic law of satisfaction (P + M = 1) and orders his organ and senses to perform little more, or
b. He allows the internal chemistry to follow its pattern and simply reject the unwanted heavy material, or
c. The process could be a combination of both.

State of Mental Synthesis

In any of the above techniques one could delay his further growth of the mind but that would be his fate and ensures, the growth is there and degradation does not happen. The preliminary knowledge of mind or the preliminary realization of organ and senses and also preliminary awareness of internal body chemistry generates a new interest in him. The new interest is again because there something good seems to appear which is not visible by the naked eyes.

But what is going in the mental synthesis are?

If he had guilt, if he was jealous, if he demanded respect, if he wandered for recognition it was his anti-mind trying to win over his mind and at this state he has already conquered over it. The present state is capable to give him MENTAL

PEACE which in knowledge or even in absence of its knowledge is a unique landmark and to be thrilled about.

It is the new developed knowledge to operate his body-mind system. It is the knowledge for operating himself through the mind and the process one has learnt is to optimize the use of organ and senses. He has minimized using the (IBC) internal body chemistry load in the internal processing and now if he optimizes the use of mental synthesis he would immediately start feeling the power which could be achieved by one, the best or the least material.

In the present scientific advanced age when machine is made to do all the labour human work he has certainly reduced the load for various organs but is important to know the effect on himself. In the developed areas or further down in that matter there would be many developed individuals who have knowingly or unknowingly reduced the load on mind for BOS due to the modern gadgets and comforts he possess but that necessarily does not take him in the higher ladder of mental level. Among these who are able to minimize sensibly (or in our present term through the mind) do feel better.

For food habits in these individuals availability would not be a constrain, there would be few among them who eat through their mind of required quantity and of the natural extract type of the diet.

People conforming to both these segments as the basic requirement for reaching higher up the mental level could still be missing the third element for optimizing the load on mental synthesis (MS). MS being not operated through the mind adds the burden on the self and the result is

- that the scope of achievement still remains for unknown, unexplainable and invisible quest of power and
- mental peace in that person still remains at a distant.

Best of food and best of material is not necessarily required but the best of knowledge and utilization of mind is that what is required and which can be adjusted to different situation around him.

In the event of availability of best of the material and best of food the majority could be under illusion as,

- As a matter of habit with available material resources in plenty you could have weakened yourself in elevation of mental growth by reducing the element of sacrifice on your own body and or
- Due to overusing mental synthesis you have lost the word 'patience' even on your own self.

But among this segment there could be few individuals who for the reason of forced circumstance necessarily had to build the sacrifice element in themselves and having no option other than have patience could get the opportunity to know the Glimpses of Power. When the rest would pity on such individuals such persons would be able to teach others that how less one needs for his body and how much he gains the power (of mind).

For the rest, the question could still remain as to why should one acquire this power?

4

THE INVISIBLE QUEST

The intellect band is another world in itself. Every human has the ingredient of it but could be failing to understand it and thus losing the opportunity to benefit of acquiring a human body in the present life. When one crosses 0.7 M level a living being comes in influencing area of Intellect band and such person has to go up in the mental ladder without his likes or dislikes. There would be many persons existing in such place in isolation. This place at the moment demands no recognition and so in their isolated state such people are contented and try to generate a calm and happy atmosphere around them. It is the process where they are still in the process of learning the new feeling which is still unexplored and explained in details to the material world irrespective of their age they belong.

For a person entering intellect band it could be new sunrise for him and others. It could be a new chapter in the present mankind and a new era. For this 0.7 M to 1.0 M is the initial stage to get the very initial information and knowledge towards that. It is also the stage when individuals would start emerging and then try to bring more in their category.

It is the perfect plan of the super creator to keep the entire universe in balance with minimum effort. The super creator had planned the living being in BRAIN band (all living being except of human) with their movement in the natural circular orbit which was capable to keep the nature in harmony itself. It is here where the same super power would have been happy with some individual because of their '*karmas*' and induced the element on MIND with one positive and one negative element to keep the system balance again.

It is the opening of channel to gradually reach the super-creator, to meet him and acknowledge him the gratitude.

It is only the '*sukarmas*' (good deeds) or positive values at every stage that would have lead him to that path. Once one acquires a mind it has only one way to rise. Doesn't matter few individual at M 0 mental level with all his karmas may go up by a fractional segment at a time.

- If such life is full of *sukarmas* it would essentially make him feel satisfied and he would affectively contributing a large segment to go up in the ladder beyond his vision of mental level. Such people who are dedicated type with minimum self-interest have contributed as a catalytic role for few others to rise further beyond the existing level and spread the newer horizon of knowledge in each steps forward.

This way when a lucky person or persons enter in the interface of *MIND* and *INTELLECT* his own built definitions of life seems to be altered. Mind band was capable to make him realize its sub branches of BOS, IBC and MS and such person now know with better clarity that mind is interacting with the sub branches rather than him. Necessarily this stage is reached by efficient utilization of each of the three branches of mind.

Human has been always in search of unhidden treasure yet unknown,

And what this treasure is?

- Utilization of his organ and senses
- Understanding and using mental synthesis
- Comfort
- Pleasure, satisfaction and contentment

All of these were the achievements but not the end.

- Lucky are those who end their life journey at these posts doing *sukarmas* in their knowledge as these individuals themselves have seen and known of the power but may have never been in position to explain others.
- Poor are those who have seen the pleasure, satisfaction from their anti-mind as their end as that would have only delayed to realise that the search is for something else and their experiment with their life falls short.

Discovery of Mental Peace

Many individuals would be lying in the interface of the Intellect band but they simply do not know about it. They are really enjoying the wealth of their mind.

- They have made a habit to follow mind and are ready for the sacrifice over their body.
- They have time and patience to obey their mind.

Resultant what they achieve is the mental peace. This *MENTAL PEACE* is the starting phenomena of the new band. Mental peace could be very wrongly interpreted by a person lying in the lower band where one may think it as an age related thing which one should ultimately achieve at a later stage of life.

Hence it is important to understand why would one achieve mental peace?

- and how?

It is when made to understand in some physical form it could percolate better in the people on lower mental level and if it happens in early age one could have a chance to see the depth in it as well. Such person would be able to relate this mental peace essentially the primary tool to discover the hidden treasure.

If in the mind band he has the capability to think, it was to discover right or wrong, positive and negative and for discovering this he had to utilize his external organ and senses. Invariably few of the organ and/or senses utilized were either more than the optimum or could be unknowingly over utilization of some portion prevented him or slowed the movement upwards towards the intellect band. The situation in the new intellect band is not the same and to reach this point it could be *his knowledge* or the *conducive situation* around him which has prevented him over-utilisation of organ and senses. In either case there is an element of his *sukarmas* to reach here and what it would mean to the person?

This would mean that he acts through the mind and has clear picture of good and bad, positive and negative for the body, organ and senses.

But what do we mean by this?

- All sorts of beautiful, ugly people are there, beautiful and ugly nature and material are there in front of our eyes.
- All sorts of soothing and irritating sound vibration are there around our ears.
- All sorts of good and bad smell are floating around the nose.

These variations are distinct and disturbing in the mental band but in the intellect band one would not be disturbed or attracted towards any of these things.

So what would happen in the intellect band?

Your eyes would appear seeing all of them, your ear would appear listening all the sound, your nose would appear smelling all of them, your hand or feet (body) would appear to be feeling all of them but recording in the intellect band would happen only which has a positive value for that stage.

But what is positive value for intellect stage?

If mind band has positive and negative value the intellect band still has positive and negative but with a difference. In the mind band positive value is the knowledge of body organ and senses and efficient utilization of all the parts whereas in the intellect band it is the knowledge of the mind which in turn operates all the ports. This is to say in this new band there is one organ as mind which has to be controlled and which in turn utilizes organ and senses as its tool for the physical work.

The mental peace in the mind and intellect interface band therefore is the gate to reach intellect and then his definition for the life starts changing. Let us take the primary element which is the basic need in the form of food,

- if in mental band for this basic need he has been wandering in wide and varied way (and in the due course creating a whole lot of mental synthesis)
- in the new intellect band his selectivity is through his mind and does not bother directly for the body.

The second most important element is security for which he has been wandering in search of various comforts.

- His aim has been to secure his body organ and senses.
- The changed definition in the new band becomes the security of the mind but could not be well known for a person in the interface of mental and intellect band.

In such a situation he may not even know that he is in the search for security of mind but certainly would know that he is in a search of an unknown element.

BUT WHY?

Because in the mind band he has been very much attached with his body organ and senses but once he would step in intellect band he would know that these elements still remains for the mechanical functioning part but their direct role is reduced or eliminated.

The primary intellect state has a similarity with the state of a child of few years but with a difference. A child of few years of age is pure at heart and mind and is still learning the art of life. He being pure and innocent does not even know about his organ and senses. If he happens to fall down while playing or running and is hurt, we could see a physical wound such as scratches over the skin but the healing is very rapid as there has been no problem. Whereas if a person at a higher mental level (where mental synthesis could have shaped within him) would have fallen down the hurt would have been more as well the recuperation. On the other hand a person in the intellect band, his state calls for complete realization of organ and senses and with the knowledge of the mind, and if the mind is in your hands (control) a physical wound would not harm and would again heal very soon.

In the state of mind one has the ability to THINK in the mental synthesis zone.

It is 'think and act' leading to rise in the mental level.

But now when mental synthesis also has to move through the mind there is not a significant act of thinking but it is optimum and positive utilization of mental syntheses.

And in doing so gives the intellect a new strength to *OBSERVE.*

Intellect now observes and act.

Observation Power Beyond the Normal Reach

Observation has been always there earlier. In fact a child by observing the parent learns experiment and explores their world. The observation has been an important part in the human progress but the logics of the mind had generally limited the observation to the reach of his organ and senses. The scientific proof calls for generating hypothesis, do a trial, make the observations and try to prove the theory.

If my eyes, ears or mind is to see it follow a rule it is proven. In the mind stage he operates within a boundary of physical nature and anything beyond if observed is not recorded from the scientific point of view and that is because of it reach in this stage. The intellect stage has a difference and the logics also starts altering here and it is the observation which one has been making in his life could be making a logic of events and seeing them coming true.

We are limiting the discussion for the worldly people living in the complexity of the human society and busy in their daily rituals for survival and so we are by no means talking of the saints who have isolated themselves from the worldly links.

This is to say a normal person would also reach the intellect band in his knowledge and that if you have reached this band and in your path with attachments and surrounding you would still come across various hurdles and complex issues,

So what?

The new state helps to give the knowledge for power of observation which in turns gives the indication to help one or indicate ones' helplessness, it would indicate to share joy or sorrow irrespective of the other person being located physically at a distant location.

The source for such observation is the organs and through the mind it percolates in the intellect to give the logic and the meaning.

In the mind band all such observations have been made and also termed as streak coincidence whereas there is no coincidencc happening but it is only the symptom which is either being recorded as a useful data for future or time is lost to stay in the lower mind band.

Let us see few examples

1. It is a tale of a holy city and where people come from far distance in their old age to die because they think that the death in that city would take them to heaven. What is the truth nobody would know but the faith of these people could be strong for themselves to be contended in their life. A man who is brought up and is working in such town and happens to see dead body being taken for cremation by a flock of people chanting God's name. Such scene becoming a regular thing does not bother his mind but he certainly picked up a habit of closing his eyes and praying to God for the departed soul (of the unknown) to rest in peace and continues for his work. With time he observes that the day he sees the dead body on his way for work [and unfailingly he bows down and remembers God for the soul to be in peace] that very day his important assignments are very successful.

One need not be in a holy place. One need not see such scene very often but similar instances could be happening to many which are personal experiences and possibiy never being shared with many with positive or negative effect in their assignments.

2. This is a story of a religious lady. She was a God fearing and a self-disciplined religious lady. Her devotion to God was in the left over time after meeting all the family obligations and so not at the cost of anybody's discomfort. When the routine family job is done she would take bath and go for her puja in her room. She had a habit to fetch prasad (dry fruits) to God and after puja distribute to whoever came. To cope with the financial condition and keep the family happy she could skip her meal but never forget to serve her God. One day the prasad is exhausted, she remembers that it has to be purchased. In the evening she goes out for a walk (a daily affair) with her husband but there is some heated argument on family matters. She can see many grocery shops being left behind in the walk but does not dare to halt and ask for purchase of dry fruits for Prasad at least that moment (which would have starved her God at least in the next morning). While returning suddenly a shopkeeper steps towards her in front of his shop and asks her politely if she needs some dry fruits [Some unknown has spoken her mind and she does take the opportunity to purchase] and her ritual of serving Prasad to the mighty God remains unbroken.

3. Best of material and best of the wealth are not the guarantee for the best of the life. Money has its own importance but let us take a situation of couple living in a nuclear family where family value and interdependence with elders is still in the mind. The lady in question is in a family way and this couple lacks social circle or thinks that way. The most trusted people are far from them at that moment and so there is worried about the process and the situation of the child birth. They could have called their dear one's but did not wanted to trouble them as they were located quite far and busy in their routine schedule. They were sure that their one's could have spent as many days they wanted but took this situation as personal problem and to face themselves. During one of the evening walks they come across an aged lady who realizing the state of this young lady says without any reference "Dear daughter you would have a son" and goes away. Boy or a girl would not have mattered but unknown lady was speaking the mind of this young lady was enough for giving momentary peace and satisfaction. Few days later she is blessed with a son and few moments later the dear one's arrive without any information to them.

4. There was a person who was quite self-confident and outwardly showed that he is not a God believer. He is time conscious and a disciplined person at home and at office. One day in a busy market as he was walking through he found a watch on the road and wanted to return to the actual owner. Further ahead he saw a bunch of young student searching something when he thought that it could be for the watch which he has found. He interacts with the students, quizzes them for the make and design etc. of the watch to confirm that it is given to the correct owner. That day is over as any normal day. Next day this gentleman had to go with his family to meet their relative to a distant town in a bus. They reached the bus stop which happened to a very crowded place. They saw a bus which was full and so waited for another bus. Another bus came and people started throwing themselves into the bus. This family man somehow pushed his children and wife one by one and finally when he entered it was packed till the footstep where he was standing. The bus started. Conductor tried to readjust the space so that all the people would come inside and are safe. This gentleman purchases the ticket and then gradually squeezes between people and reaches where his other family members have found a place where three of his people are sitting cramped in a seat of one. Irrespective finally finding them together and heading for the destined place was good enough to bring the smile among them. Suddenly this gentleman finds that his wrist watch is missing, he remembers the pull and push while boarding and standing for long on the footstep and thought that some body has pick pocketed or otherwise it has fallen out of bus. He remembers to see his wallet and find it in its place. Even in the jam packed bus he makes attempt to reach back where the conductor sits, informs that he has lost a watch. Immediately conductor takes out from his pocket and says that this watch has been found on the footstep. Take it. No further argument, it was his watch; he collects it and is happy.

The watch could not have been the costliest item to disturb but a time conscious person who has selflessly helped was immediately rewarded in the similar field and had enough to enlighten him who has become a big devotee of God and a very good human being.

5. A father had a well self-disciplined timid son. The son was brought up in a much protected atmosphere and the child is introvert so could have developed that thinking in his father. The son completes graduation and gets an employment as well. He is not very satisfied with the job which he shares with his father. The son who has not travelled his own and not taken many risks and when he has newly employed does not know how he would go for an interview and what explanation he would give. His father reads his weak personality and says to his son that he should inform him about the call whenever it happens and his father would send him a message for the sickness of his mother to relive him for the job. The situation arrives, the son informs father about the interview and gets back the message for sickness and so the interview is done and the son is selected also. The son changes the job but soon his father falls sick and leaves the body.

What a truth? If only we can understand when the mind is speaking the truth we could start knowing many more mysteries. Everyone does experience sometime that he or she has said something good or bad in a casual talk and it has come out to be true exactly.

6. A senior gentleman working in railways was travelling on a train. As the train was whistling through a thick of forest one night this gentleman peeking in the direction of train moving he saw someone waving a flag to stop the train. He thought in the dark it has some illusion but again peeped out again he saw the same thing. His mind didn't settle and after repeated viewing the same thing he asked the train driver to halt. What he saw was amazing, few yards ahead where the train was halted the rail track was found to be opened. The disaster was averted. More than that the gentleman was sure that he saw the mighty God and on returning whatever he was wearing he distributed to the needy ones as the prasad of the God.

These are all real incidents of different kind. Some appear to have greater impact and some could be seen with not much significance *to the second person,* but the person concern if is observant and in the appropriate mental level would record them without projecting to others.

One thing common among the different person who had these different experiences were that all were self-disciplined people. All these could not be in the intellect level or reaching to the intellect level but if such incidents are recorded by any individual and they help them in transformation (realization) one certainly is rising in the mental level from their existing base.

These few samples are indicative but in actual life everyone comes across very often in their life path for good or bad cause but the affect would vary as,

- The people lying in the lower mental level do not observe them at all,
- Little higher level there are some who notice as coincidence but do not record them in their mind whereas
- There is yet another lot who record these incidences and then after their repetition in different context surely believe them not to be coincidence. This again is the indication for one to be entering higher mental level towards the intellect band.

The role of *karmas* come again in forefront and make it clear that one's destiny is not in his own hand but has influence on his deeds past and present.

- If one's life has been full of negative *karmas* (including yester life) one is bound to repent in physical form in this world. Such people if come across bad coincidences it would indicate that even if they think and want to reform themselves they would not reach near the intellect band as of now and would be far below in mental level.
- But another individual whose earlier *karmas* were moderate to good and does observe the coincidences he could be able to co-relate them for the positive end and would be able to lift his mental level.

One who generates a primary knowledge of such coincidences starts knowing that there is some power superior to the mind. He would be able to relate the incidences with his body organ and senses by the act of seeing, feeling or thinking which is a very important turning point in the making of observations.

The question generates within him now is *HOW IT HAPPENED?*

If in the mind band it was the question "WHY" which use to be generated for the individuals quest but in the interface and in the intellect band the question becomes "HOW". The question HOW would allow him to rise gradually clarifying step by step each small thing but in different fashion. Reaching intellect band itself envelops a person with *invisible power* which one may not be knowing but gives the knowledge of coincidences beyond the physical reach of his organ and senses.

Intellect Band in the Reach

Mental band in the range of 0.7 and 1.0 M has great importance to play in future. There is no such ingredient or value that does not exist in any human being at any point of time. It is only with evolving nature of human being he is able to identify and give a new name with new experience. We have already said that a person who is lying between 0.5 M and 0.7 M

- has acquired realization of BOS (Body organ and senses)

- and is in a better aware state for IBC (Internal body chemistry) and by the time he reaches 0.7 M he would have realization of this element as well and
- has acquired a good knowledge of MS (mental synthesis).

Between 0.7 and 1.0 M he has to realise about IBC in totality and then gradually improve the awareness about MS.

Total realization of MS would mean a great achievement but at the moment in this present material world if at all that would take much more time for any individual to be in such a position. At the moment even reaching near its vicinity would be an eye opening to the people and could become a guide to follow the path.

The coincidences mentioned are the starting symptoms for the mind to be more aware for MS and hence mentioned as starting symptoms for intellect band. Such incidences give the idea about the interaction in intellect band. Once you have the faith in this it would start pushing towards the realization. At the moment you donot know your capability to share joy or sorrow with your beloved persons irrespective where they are situated and the faith would gradually tune you with this invisible power.

What is intellect band?

If we understand the role of intellect band as we have discussed the mental band the functional differences could be clearer. In the mind band utilization of organ and senses had the limit of its reach to its physical extent in all aspects viz. seeing, hearing, tasting, smelling and feeling. In the intellect band his reach is extends beyond the physical reach through the same organs, senses and with the addition of MS. One may understand as transfer of mental power but actually it is the intellect observing and the mind interacting.

We also know that one has reached such higher state in the mind band primarily due to optimum utilization of his organ and senses which he is still following as a habit and this extended state calls for further optimum utilization of MS as well.

The active distribution network in the intellect band for the day to day work is controlled as,

1. There is no anti-mind existing as one has crossed in Intellect band. While in the interface region one could be forced to the circumstance around him to bring back the anti-mind which could be due to his *karmas* and would hold that individual to go forward.
2. For immediate physical need in all the departments directly mind is controlling.
3. The new element born as intellect is able to see the invisible air, light and sound waves and sense the situation far beyond and informs the mind at the cost of the load that mind would be doing otherwise for immediate physical need.

These invisible waves would be interfacing with people in the lower band as well but becomes irrelevant as the person situated does not have any clue about it and the truth is far beyond his capacity.

The question could crop up why one should go up in the ladder and the answer would be that,

- We did not want to climb up in the mental ladder but we have progressed. We did not want because we had no knowledge about it.
- Similarly it would be the natural progression to go up in the search of the ultimate truth.

As we have no knowledge at the moment the question could crop up of 'why' but does not have relevance.

It should be known that in a huge population only selected go ahead. After many years few among such have the leadership to impart the knowledge and try to inculcate in the lower mass. Hence the general human people do rise but with a great lag of time.

Considering the world today we would have human with mental level of all the fractional levels from 0.0 M level to 0.5 M level in abundance. As we go up the lower group could be becoming narrower but does not diminish. As the mind band has anti-mind element also all these sub-fractional part are further split with varying mind and anti-mind proportion making the scene complex in a society they live.

But the person leading does not have any such problem otherwise he would have never reached such a position. It is also the role of his *sukarmas* in yester life woven with *sukarmas* in the present one which guides one in this direction. It is the knowledge of the intellect power one has smelled or seen that he does not want to loose and does not want to differ whether he is staying in a palace or staying in a hut. The attachment with the new power facilitates in making his mind more aware and in turn realise for its sub activities of BOS, IBC and MS. Now what he needs and would practice is the optimum utilization of mind functions and for which he would start further sacrifice on himself to reduce the load on his mind.

Role of *Karma* and the Fate Element

What is written above is significantly important to understand as this stage is for the knowledge of preliminary level of a new human within him. The story is of human who has a family, has a social and the unwarranted environment around him and so we are not by any chance talking of special power of a person living in isolation away from the worldly affairs. How could one reach this level?

Human living in man-made society would tend to go towards the acquiring the intellect state when he is able to satisfy the above definition of optimum utilizing the faculties of the mind. The habit for the reduction of load on mind would come in different ways and there would be an evolutionary progress but the easiest path would be to reduce the negativity in one's knowledge. If we remember 0.7 M stage portion anti-mind is reduced one but it would remain till one has reached 1.0 M level and hence one's work is only to try to scrap the residual anti-mind. In the physical level the basic meaning would be that,

- 'I' would not see evil, not do any evil, not eat any poison (unwanted to body), not touch evil nor feel any evil.

- 'I' would not speak any evil not think any evil.
- It also means that 'I' would not overdose the organs by their respective duty to strain the mind.

All this trait calls for self-discipline and restrain from many activities which one could categorize in their routine and justifying their act. Justification is good for scientific process, it does not have an important place if one is comparing to someone else because justification itself would mean that one is doubtful of the process or action and which further would mean that there is clash within oneself between his mind and anti-mind. Till this doubt remains one is far from reaching the point near intellect level but even if this fact is understood there is a chance that there is a scope for an attempt.

Let us see how one's *karmas* play a role in the process which would make understand that the destiny is beyond one's direct effort and is controlled from somewhere else.

There are two good human beings Mr.A and Mr.B at the cross road of 0.7 M level. As both have reached at this position by their knowledge and experience they try to avoid any negativity in their life in their knowledge.

Considering the work of only one organ that is eye both of them understand that they should not see anything bad and thus not show anything bad and also not overburden the eyes. Let us observe one day's schedule of each who get up in the morning, go to their work place, come back home and call a day.

Mr.A gets up in the morning. Takes bath and picks up the newspaper to flip the news. He sees the headlines of terrorist attacks and killing, he further reads the story of a rape somewhere. Completes his breakfast and moves for the office in his car. On the way he notices collision of two vehicles (and thinks for a moment that some would be hurt) but continues to his destination. From office he has to go to a workshop and there he sees the labor trouble in a section who are fighting and using abusive language. The heated arguments going on do not relate to the part he is visiting and so he is not interested to know more about it. He returns back home relaxes and opens television for some relaxation. Violence and sex are the ingredients that come before his eyes and finally he retires for the day.

Mr.B similarly gets up in the morning. Takes bath and lifts the newspaper and flips the sports page to see that one of football team has won the match whom he favored. Rushes to the office and is nicely greeted by his colleagues. He has to company few more to another place for an official assignment and while going they cross through a lush green place appear as a paradise. Had a successful meeting and returned home. His children greet him with smile and also give a news for some award they have won at school. In the late evening he spends some time before television and listen some debate going on and sees some adventure scene being shown in one of the channel. His satisfied day comes to an end to greet another day.

In these two cases Mr.A has strained his eyes right from the morning till late night. His involvement was not there in any of the act but unknowingly and without his wish or desire he has been seeing the sex, violence, death etc. in different places which are all negative in nature and are occupying a useful area of the mind otherwise. Whatever Mr.A has seen all through the day he has not only strained his eyes but also strained his useful part of the mind depriving him to reach and relish the intellect approaching stage. These were the hurdles of self *karmas* which prevented or delayed him to rise. Whereas Mr. B whose past *karmas* in store were healthy did not meet with such incidences.

The unique incidents and coincidences if observed carefully and registered in their mind would allow anyone to rise in their mental level from their existing stage which could be as low as 0.3 M level. Observation and registering would mean that one is able to make one more disciplined in the process. However in the above example where Mr.A and B are at the cross road of 0.7 M level and from the point of view of an average person in today's world both the persons are situated where mental peace is the present target. By the karmic process the former one unknowingly is delaying in realizing more about his organ and senses through his mind and the result is that person A is away from the mental peace whereas the later one gets the opportunity to see beyond the targeted goal.

The example we have given for one external organ and it holds true for all the separate organs external and internal which in short are also linked with mental synthesis.

Intellect Band and the Physical Organs

Few individuals have always been in the intellect band and even further up but in the general process of evolution unless the message is clearly known to specifically one large group of human we can not say that this level is reached. In fact there would come a time when step by step people would reach and would know the art to sustain it. The action of intellect band does happen also in the higher mental band in isolation.

Another point of consideration is the physical organs which would be there in any band but with a difference. Movements of physical organs are visible and are necessary for the survival and are the key which as they are visible to self and others.

What could be the intellect influence to the organs?

Let us take an example of mouth as the organ concern.

The mouth and the mental synthesis have a great significance in the primary intellect band and thus important for a person in higher stage of mental level who has still to crack upon the residual anti-mind. At this stage the anti-mind relates to the mental synthesis activities and so there could be two type situation prevailing as below of Mr. A and Mr. B,

1. Mr. A utilizes his mouth extensively and is termed as extrovert and frank. Generally he being a good and honest person he is also termed as practical. Could be that he is able to influence a greater number of other human being but do we know within himself what is happening?

Because of the nature developed he talks a lot and sometimes negative also. The over-utilization of the function is done at the cost of unbalancing his internal body chemistry (IBC) and mental synthesis (MS). Such a person may reach the intellect band and achieve the mental peace but certainly is away from the knowledge of the power (of I band).

2. Mr. B on the other hand who has reduced the anti-mind has learnt the art of speaking less or speaking only useful content that he thinks are important to share with other. He continues to talk less and try to operate through the mind. He does talk less and whatever he says generally happens. This empowers his observation he is able to see the other's mind and accordingly does not speak that would hurt the other person. It is not that he cares to what he says (caring is the habit one has to cultivate much earlier to reach this stage) but his mind make him speak which comes true in the actual world.

These traits are the powers which can be observed and brought in practice for the welfare of others. When reaslied to this level one knows that there is very little requirement for oneself and so the enjoyment is more when it could be shared with others. This process would bring many more in similar elevated category with time to come where unknowingly his contribution would be there (that is a selfless cause).

Each organ thus would be observed to have added power and it would be observed by the person who has been miserly using his specific organs in reaching this stage.

Characteristic of the Intellect Band and the Movement Ahead

The entrance of the intellect band is possible only after unclothing of physical self and so after throwing the ego embedded within. If one had earlier the sense of attachment with his dear and near ones, his kith and kins and with other materials he does shed the physical sense of attachment but that does not imply to isolate physically. When the knowledge of mind signifies the associated power it becomes immaterial for him or run away or live together.

As it was always a challenge to live with assorted people and elevate the mental level here again the real challenges is tasted by a person living in the present social structure and happily relish this new stage. This is only the process that would guide others to glance beyond for the newer discovery.

Mental peace is automatically there at this stage but what we understand by these words of mental peace?

It is a state where nothing much good or bad would disturb him. Good or bad would not create any anxieties in him. He knows the mental attachment with his blood relations, close friends and relatives, job associates and neighbors all the time. Now it is his intellect that informs him about the well being of your people and further responds and acknowledges to them from their point of view of joy or sorrow.

Such a person in a normal course is a self-disciplined person. Self-disciplined in all the activity zones of the mind which are BOS, IBC and MS. Naturally he shows the physical discipline to others with a positive approach. He has to keep following this to retain the strength of intellect and develop a nature accordingly. As people do exist in this stage today without knowing (or knowing subjectively) has a historic significance,

Why we call it a historic significance is that on the day majority has not even reached 0.7 M level and the population spectrum is spread to all the fractional levels below that. The majority may not have reached 0.7 M landmark in the natural course of life and even many would be reaching around in their last stages of life could not be helping others. But the positive achievers have reached much ahead and already paved the path. Such early achievers to step forward in the mental level were never recognized and would never be as they would have no proof to express their knowledge and pleasure in physical form which another person has not tasted.

Still it does not stop one to rise up as there is a self sense of achievement without hurting any other body and is also a natural way to climb the ladder.

Once a person has stepped in the intellect band there is no way to stop here and so they would continue to rise in the quest for invisible power more and more. Isolated individuals would be deriving pleasure of this unknown power but when individual would be establishing this stage with more knowledge and strength they would try to envelop such power to their kith and kins. Such individuals with their kith and kins would then tend to form a collective group which would have similarity to the tribal people in the mental stage we know in the early era of civilization. This intellect tribe thus formed would be very different and would exist with other lower format of the mental stage. This would highlight new values and the strength associated.

There would be still hundreds and hundreds of years left to reach the place and so does not have higher significance. But one thing is sure that further evolution would have similarity of profile of the present one and important features would be the followings:

1. Development of human values would be in the similar form where the love value would remain the core and most important one.
2. The logics would be changed. The logic in mental stage would appear very meager which best could generate a physical body or achievements whereas in this band the higher logics would come up and mental achievements would generate which at present we can think only as a fiction.
3. As mental band (M) is associated with mind and anti-mind and it is anti-mind leading in illusion to identify the truth, similarly in intellect band (I), it is mental power associated with intellect and anti-intellect and anti-intellect will be the cause to delude the truth further to the majority.

The intellect level is not the ultimate. If power is seen

and subsequently utilized in day to day activity the positive movers would go ahead in search of the source of the power as the ultimate truth.

Higher intellect level could be not of immediate interest but all the symptoms are well experienced by different people in the existing band in pieces which keeps the quest live to know more. The intellect band as said is not the ultimate stage and is only where the taste of the power is known. The source of the power would remain the quest further. For that let us understand the intellect band in physical details.

Physical Interpretation of Intellect Level

It is easy to understand any subject if it is explained physically. It could be our limitation in the existing mental band nevertheless gives the opportunity for its interpretation to a wider section.

Let us go back to the fig. 2.1 part-2 which was as below,

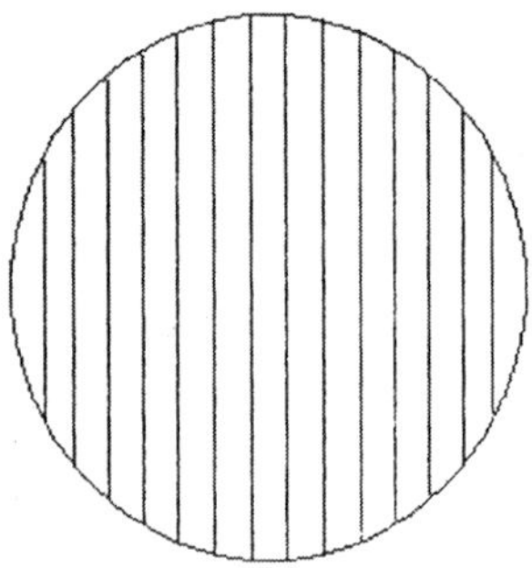

STATE-2

Fig. 4.0

This figure represents the mental level of 1.0 M which we have not reached generally. This state is achieved by conquering the physical elements within us and complete recognition of the mind. We had also used the term of mental orientation. The mental orientation in the brain band was in circular loops which were broken and gradually stretched deformed and reformed to make it symmetric or asymmetric. The above figure is the ultimate most symmetric orientation possible in this band where anti-mind is totally eliminated.

If the physical activities are still being carried out by the person it is not the brain, it is not the anti-mind but the intellect is getting done by the mind as a tool.

Refer fig. 4.1 below.

The basic three elements remain the same that is BOS, IBC and MS. Eliminating the anti-mind (the negative element) one has reached the state as depicted in 4.1A. As numbers of activities are still being carried out by a person even though through the mind each activity is representing a straight line and so there is a cluster of parallel lines.

The intellect sense gives the knowledge of all the operations being carried out are by the mind as a single organ which in turns get the job done by respective tools of physical organs that we understand. The intellect is keen in its observations and continues to enrich its power.

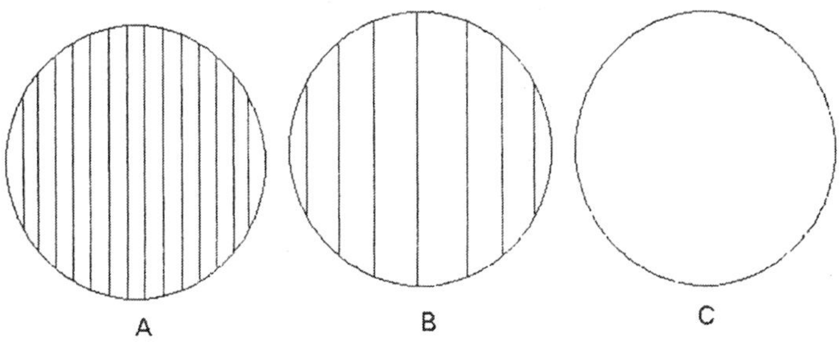

Fig. 4.1

In the preliminary stage he is already seeing how the power is making the objectives fulfill and thus knows that he would have to be more observant by lessening its interaction with the mind. This may further show that that the reduction of BOS, IBC and MS confirming that what he needs for is living is very little food and may lose the position of priority as in the mind band. Reduction of food would also reduce the reduction of IBC automatically. MS does not play a role of thinking which is the prime force in the mind band to uplift him to this stage. If required by the intellect MS could put up a question 'WHY' but in all the other regular activities he knows the reality (which is different and understood by a person in the mind band) thus has now improved observation power. The similarity between the stages in mind and intellect band is something like,

- in the mind band the thinking power was active and it was like an audio cassette whereas
- in the intellect band the observation power is like audio and video cassette which he has started operating in his limited knowledge at the moment.

It is the experience and the knowledge of a person about the invisible power that he would like to retain so to keep his mind active for the happenings beyond his physical reach. He retains it and is able to share it till it is not misutilised. At this preliminary stage if he uses his organ and senses to express the intellect signals on mind the result is not obeying the intellect and the outcome is the disappearance of the power.

In *Ramayana* there are whole lot of *devas* and *asuras* who had such power and could be the ultimate ripe stage in the evolution of the process. In the epic there is one weapon by the name of *Brama-astra* which could tie and arrest any other person but the weapon lost its power if any other weapon touches the affected person.

Similarly the invisible power is the power attained by a person by his living habits and who has reached the intellect stage automatically meaning has put a restrain on using the mind properties of BOS, IBC and MS. The role of *karmas* continuously play with him. If his karma is responsible to bring till this stage his present behavior is responsible for his path forward. Properties around intellect band are of similar type as they are around the mind band. The foremost basic hurdle in the mind has been 'comparison' and a huge lot of people are still unable to cross over and are trapped and delay their evolutionary growth. Similarly 'comparison' is the primary hurdle in the growth in the intellect band but with the difference. One who is able to put constrain over the mental activities and thus keep the load of organ and senses reduced is able to reach the stage shown in fig.4.1 B with parallel lines and one plays more with his mind and organ and senses delays the rise in the ladder.

i. In the case of mind band reduction in mental synthesis was done by maneuvering BOS and IBC whereas in the case of intellect band it would be possible by playing with the mind as a single organ.
ii. In the mind band he was dependent on his BOS and IBC to perform various types of (physical) activities internal and external for his living whereas the essential activities would continue but the physical exertion is reduced as it becomes dependant and as instructed by the mind.

This description is for entering the intellect band and thus are the initial symptoms which would appear and disappear in absence of the truth known to the people and inability to explain to the (so called) learned of today who understand the logics invented which would follow quite a time later in the time.

The fact we have progressed in the mind band and the leaders were those who had reduced the load on the mind and the body, who had optimally used their energy (with or without their knowledge about it) or equating the primary equation of P+M=1 in very small steps. We might not know this and thus not acknowledge it and give the credit to the one we see as powerful physically, financially, technologically etc. but that is due to our present limitation where one can not agree to anything that is physically not seen or brought into existence.

At the cross road (M into I band) the climbing up the ladder the law of reduction of the load would continue. The mind may demand for further dietary changes or else would sacrifice some of the activities of the organ and senses. This phenomenon would unknowingly make him reach where he would find a definite strength developed. Primary strength could be an isolated strength developed specifically of the body - organ - senses which has been sacrificed more.

Say for an example a positive and constructive person in his regular disciplined activities happens to be very busy to abstain the touch sense far more than the minimum required at his elevated level. Such a person would develop the strength in his touch that could do wonders. For more clear understanding let us know,

What is a touch sense?

Hand shake is a touch sense, kissing is a touch sense, patting is a touch sense. Eating by your hand would not contribute or contribute very less in that way. The effect on mind by the touch good or bad has the implication consumes the energy not realized by a normal person.

In the intellect band such activities are operating through the mind as and when required to maintain the peace of mind. One could have made the habit for continuously abstaining the touch for his reasons and circumstances but to such a person touch could then lead to the distraction of the peace.

What could one has got strength in such a case – he could know the role of unknown power of intellect and his touch – Such person has to be human caring and when he touches (knowingly the essential need for it) the problem, the anxieties of another human are immediately eliminated. It might sound like a magic or fiction but it is not so. If we come across a person at this platform we might call him enlightened and his act as miracle in absence of much proved logic present. There have been persons in isolation still would be present but are rare at present to confirm the theory of time ahead.

Such incidence would only highlight the awareness of the invisible power attained by one in physical form for one of the sense. This power can not be utilized for the fun sake at this stage. Using the power even for essential positive requirement the person would loose the ability to climb but his job could have been over and transferred to someone else down the line. On the other hand if the invisible power is mis-utilised by one he would only be ensuring to move in the negative direction of destruction of self including many others.

The quest would be now to acquire the knowledge to capture more of the invisible power in more and more activities of his body-organ-senses. *The steady and gradual rise would be in the fashion human have developed tribes, colonies and the bigger recognized states that we know.

** Refer my book "The Evolving Human And The Future World" for the mental evolution where development of tribes, colony and the country are explained and they all fall in the mind band of today.*

The guru is great (selfless and satisfied) if among his thousand disciples atleast one is able to reach farther than he has been taught. Such gurus would always be there as the design of the superior power though not in the physical limelight. As said in the above paragraph when one uses the invisible power even for the positive or constructive reason one would tend to lose it but in the process either two would develop such power or one would develop even higher power.

5

THE INVISIBLE POWER

The Invisible power is not the creator but the tool of the creator to keep the universe in balance. He has germinated the mind in human to understand and reach back to him. The creator is not male or female, he is not good or bad but his tool has the ingredient of duality. Below the mind band (animal and vegetation) there is a self-balancing method of destruction and existence but from the mind band the natural balance ceases to exist. To neutralize the effect he has developed good and bad like two things. In the mind band there is duality, in the intellect band which has to come in future also has the duality ingredient. The duality can not be removed completely in the human form but whoever early or late in the life is able to reduce it is able to understand it better. The more you reduce the clear is the vision.

The interpretation of the invisible power in this advanced age in the mind band can be gauged by the same term of power. One is said to be on the higher stature who has higher physical power, higher financial power, higher technological power and these physical power would one day educate more about the invisible power when all the existing such power would fail to keep the system in control.

In the present situation of the world the population of the human is increasing but the number of humans near the intellect band are very less. If it is so why at all is that more important to talk about them or even follow them. An average person is only capable to follow an identity or follow a leader. As on today even if a person is able to observe the world beyond his physical reach, another person would give a word of fantasy for such thought and would not mean much to him. The real recognition of the primary intellect power would only appear when the present physical power (in the form of economics and authority) would cause a fatal accident resulting a large devastation. It is not that at this stage a person with intellect power would step in for a savior deed. But infact when the human devastation and the unfavorable environment would still not affect those in this band shall automatically be brought in the limelight and would be recognized inspite their own wishes. It is only the matter of destiny that in search of the invisible power one attains a physical power and is distracted and stagnates his progress from the future path towards the creator.

With the speed the world is moving ahead it might not be more than 8 to 10 generation (or less) when the physical power would come at stake and is challenged by the invisible power by some.

Majority of human race does not move upward in the mind band but everytime more of them would appear below their elevated level without their own knowledge of their goal to acquire the invisible power. From this heap of human a small fraction that step upward are again trapped on their path and deviate from the goal. In deviation not only they loose a single lifetime opportunity to be proud of their human life but are also unable to understand and utilize and tap the potential that is nowhere else but within them. In the process a pyramid is formed of the human race with different status on mental evolution.

The Human Pyramid for the Ultimate Quest

The fig. 5.0 shows the human pyramid being formed in their evolutionary process. The pyramid has three sections marked as B, M, I and O :

i. Section between B and M is the section in the lowest

stage and would include animal, vegetation and some human as well.

ii. Section between M and I are critical for us. Almost all of the human exist in this area.

iii. Section between I and O has to emerge. Few human could be lying in this area but are not recognized at the moment.

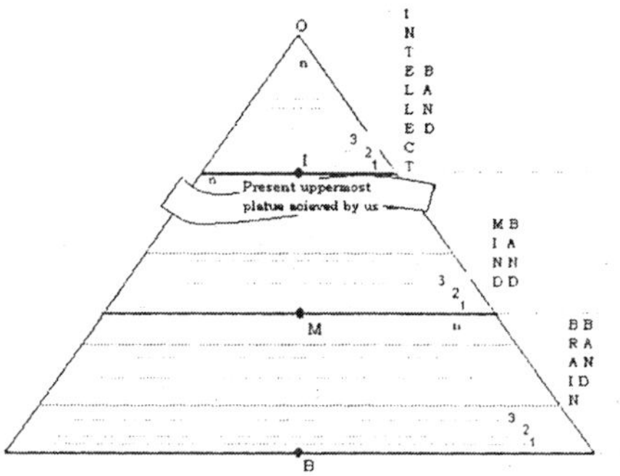

Fig. 5.0

Each of these sections can be further divided into number of sub-sections. In the figure sub-layer are marked in different parallel lines as 1, 2, 3 ..... n.

As we climb up the ladder of Mind and further to Intellect the passage is becoming narrower. It is an invisible quest for anybody at point M unknowingly to go up in the thinking ladder of the Mind and few could be lucky to reach the destiny 'I'.

But this has not stagnated and fulfilled them as the path ahead is wide open to reach the point 'O' and that may take couple of thousands of year more.

Our topic is on self and so we would limit our discussion with reference to self rather than global affect. All the way we have been focusing on the positive side of the self which has enabled a human to rise in the mental ladder. What is not described in the detail is that each minute step from M to I shown there are infinite subdivisions marked as 1,2,3,4

.......n in the figure. The bulk of human end up going away from the path in early or later stage of life. We have discussed about the negative parameters where one tends to get entangled in the self made cobweb which are of physical nature operating from anti-mind.

The behavior of path ahead between M and I would follow in the similar fashion with difference of main ingredients. There would be 1,2,3,4 ...... n subdivisions between the two stages and it would be negative traits as the hurdle for all to rise ahead. The basic difference in the ingredient would be its nature which would change from physical to mental.

Before 'I' band the path blocking ingredient has been the physical nature whereas after 'I' band the path blocking ingredient would be of mental nature. In mental stage the negative traits described are the word such as comparison and jealousy are the easiest words to attract anybody in power. People want to have physical power in their area of living. The aim to accumulate wealth is again a physical power by which one could assume to keep physically safe. The comparison and the jealousy which create the barrier are also of the physical nature. If comparison has been the smallest or the primary negative trait of physical nature this comparison has been attached all the way with evolution at each step. In fact comparison has been a good scientific tool as a bench marking on the scientific things and a ladder to develop and improve further. Same comparison in the human being has been the value to disturb the peace within oneself and also surrounding. At a superior and elevated stage in M level one could think of economic independence with the hope that lot of wealth could satisfy them and keep safe and if the goal has been only wealth the satisfaction ends up very soon. But if the wealth is a side effect of the work and dedication towards it, the meaning could be different and beyond a point (wealth) could have no meaning for that human being. In case the accumulated wealth does not change the meaning it is the greed of superior order and one is trying to seek some (physical) power in his territory of the industry, area of his community or a nation. All these powers at different stages could be easily understood as the capability of mind and the strength lies in it.

Intellect Span

To understand about 'I' band proper understanding of M band is necessary. As the functioning of M band is mentioned in details certain aspects would bring the clarity for similarity and the difference in the band before and after M.

Intellect span in the figure is starting from 'I' and ends to O. As to rise from B to M it has taken a long time with steps of

i. Knowledge,

ii. Awareness,

iii. Skill and

iv. Realization

about the living being at large, about the body organ, senses and the mind and the capability of self from the physical perspective and that was the limit of this band.

It is always that what is inside one's mind one sees it, what is in one's mind he does it rather than reverse. The result of the action could be in favour of or not (good or bad) but most of the people have in mind to win or to lose, to accept or to reject and the more anti-mind they possess the clarity of the vision is poorer.

Entering 'I' band has one important landmark that anti-mind has minimized (becomes zero) and one has attained due to his own effort of many lives and disciplined life in the present one. Making anti-mind zero means one has conquered body organ and senses and has a good control over mind.

**By the phrase" conquered body organ sense" it should not be understood that one has become saint and left the worldly affairs. Living being does require certain inputs to move on and fulfillment of those are essential.*

This would mean that a person's physical greed have

come down and one is utilising his body organs and senses with minimum care. But how does he do? And what is the effect?

But how does he do?

M band has been the area of duality with mind and anti-mind in different living beings in different proportion leading to different behavior and different results. In all the circumstances it was playing with organ and senses and the mind factor (mind or anti-mind). It was the energy that was used in each action and energy destroyed to look beyond. M band having unique property to use body organ and sense limits itself in physical parameter for everything be it natural or man-made thing. The physical aspect is so strong that the energy that of otherwise satisfied and fulfilled person thinks of power (in physical form) but does not realize what is instigating such feeling.

On the other hand people who have saved their energy for whatever the reason and their background have reduced the anti-mind would have seen a power (a different power) which generates satisfaction in them of much higher order. They would sense that this power is the source giving the energy to their system and so the quest could begin again to understand and know about this power.

It is interesting to note that in today's advanced world knowledge of yoga is being accepted and used by many. Yoga or exercise of body and mind would have affect and allow one to forget the daily worry for a moment and relax a person. It could help in balancing the equation, P+M=1 to give the satisfaction but such person would have exercised (physically) to use much energy to be deprived of having the knowledge of the power (within). Nevertheless noble soul from such lot are the gurus to guide the rest to find out whatever they missed or understood too late.

In M band each action which the body organ and senses make along with the instruction of mind and anti-mind utilizes energy of different type. The energies are negative and positive and overall effect is on the self which could hamper to move ahead in the mental level. Whereas if the anti-mind is zeroed down and one enters 'I' band he has total control over his mind. We have said earlier that mind does not act anything negative and thus in such circumstance a man in 'I' band gives the instruction to the mind to do the rest. Any action of body organ and senses thus are the affect of the instruction of the mind and the energy thus consumed is negligible or *nil.

**In the beginning of the essay we have mentioned the effect on eye for a 3 years old child and an older person viewing a television for a longer duration. The child who laughs on a comic does not tire oneself as energy consumed is minimum whereas the older one who is engrossed in the emotion has greater impact and consumes more energy.*

It means apparently person in 'I' band would appear innocent like a child but highly knowledgeable and aware and realized to others around.

Operating through mind would mean all the actions for surviving is bound in discipline. Eating as much required and what is essential is taken which could sharpen the new area of power which is in the scope of his understanding. And so each activity of a person is redefined in a altered format that does not exhaust his energy more than required at the minimum level.

And what is the effect?

Entry in the intellect band would appear painful for a person who is in the midst of M band and the early birds to reach are the unknown and unrecognized people as it is not their demand but are ahead of such physical requirements. As the world churns and the luck of such people would get the recognition even if they do not want. The recognition could hamper the individual for their further growth but that would be their destiny and the design of the power which we are going to see further.

A minimum recognition of one would make a very big difference and would throw a new light even in science of tomorrow. It would start an evolution process within the evolved system where the definitions of the human requirements and the resources of the self would start changing.

If the effect of saving the energy would bring one closer to a new power it would mean that he is able to use the physical activities much beyond the reach of body organ and senses (which the mind was doing in its physical approach).

i. One would be able to see much beyond a pair of eyes can see.

ii. One would be able to hear much beyond a pair of ears can do.

And would be same for all the other organs.

Not limiting to the external organs the internal chemistry would also change with modified requirement to keep the energy load reduced. The physical greed would reduce.

Such status could be attained by a wealthy or not so wealthy person but availability of material does not hamper necessarily. At the moment if we consider God as a hypothetical character who is away from any form of greed but if he has to look after his creation he has to have or potential to give the basic necessity to the person to grow. Similarly a person who has the knowledge of power (within) and wants to benefit the other would find a place of comfort (physical) as observed by others though it would make not a much sense as this time and devotion would be used for others.

It would mean that they would be taken as the real rulers of the new society (gradually it would translate from guiding to rule by the people because of the quality others have observed). With one recognition more would follow and gradually there would start the duality zone in the 'I' band with a difference and similarity.

The difference would be the content of knowledge and the similarity would be the loss to rise ahead to what we have seen and observed in the 'M' band.

The development of science also would take place in the new area which has limited at present for the fact unless physically tested. It should be known that any scientific fact starts from a hypothesis which is arbitrary and comes in shape when one scientist brings out what is in his mind by the scientific tools and so when such power within would crop in the scientist they would generate a new method to prove with whatever boundary requirements it calls for. Before scientific finding and after the findings the nature has been behaving similarly but the knowledge is changing the mind and the pattern of living. Mind and the living pattern are two independent things and a person in 'I' band would know that living pattern does not necessarily governs the mind but it is the person's own capability to conquer himself in any condition. New science would throw more light on this.

We would not like to go in details as this would make all hypothetical at the moment but in nut shell the hierarchy with duality in 'I' would generate the remaining amount of the pyramid of the fig. 5.0 to reach the top 'O'.

If at a point 'I' a human could be said above the physical self it is only the body organ senses, internal body chemistry and the mental synthesis which he does not bother but does care for the mind which is instructing for the rest. The stage O ideally would be where one would go above the self, above the level to operate through the mind and what would operate such a person would be the *"Invisible power"*.

Only one person would be able to reach the top stage who would be in a position to see and talk with the God. The creator of the mysterious world and universe. This would seem to be fantasy as on the day. The God or the creator would not be like a human and so difficult to realize. It is not important to understand about the God but his small power which is governing the system so cleverly, we would see that in the next chapter.

For a moment if we accept the theory the great epic *Mahabharata* war was the era of the peak of the pyramid (fig. 5.0) with very clear indication about it.

Referring the small episodes of the *Mahabharata*

i. The war was fought with different type of arms like

missiles and jets but more superior in character. In Mind band (where we exist) we can only have the best weapon of physical in nature and so could have man-made weapons whereas in 'I' band it is possible to have a combination of man-made weapons with weapons operated by mental power (instead of physical power).

ii. It was not television or computer giving the first hand information of the war to Sanjay to narrate to *Dhritrashtra*, it was extra sense or the invisible powering in much elevated 'I' band to catch the audio and video signals beyond the physical limits to narrate the story to the king.

iii. It was the power of the eyes of *Gandhari* (which were not used as she lived blinding it) which was capable to make the Duryodhan's body like a steel for his protection.

It was only one person KRISHNA who could touch the point 'O' and one who had total invisible power that we would never be able to know but could try to have a vision or ability to fictionalize it.

We in this era are following an identical path and have not even before reached the point 'I' have started bothering to save the planet. We have started bothering about nature, the jungle, the environment and the population and so on. We have still to cross one-third portion and that would take hundreds or thousands of more years.

But than what is the equation?

And what does happen? And what is our control?

What should one do?

There are innumerous such questions generated immediately.

If the path is straight up and the time is defined (which actually is so) it makes itself clear that the destiny is well defined and nothing much is in one's hand except for one in his knowledge and capacity to keep on doing the action (*karma*) and optimally utilizing his body organ and senses, internal chemistry and mental synthesis and later on the 'mind' to make the action (*karma*) as *sukarma* (positive action).

But what good is there by doing the sukarmas?

One would ask for more when he would know that *sukarma* would add the values like 'element of sacrifice', generating patience which would minimizing the self.

The answer is simple that such a person would be contributing his tiny power in reaching the higher altitude and reaching face to face with THE CREATOR.

The Creator and the Creation

The scientists have revealed many mysteries in our world and which have led to different type of innovations. They have probed about the earth, under the water and above the earth also. They are continuously probing the stars in our galaxy and have knowledge that there are many such galaxies. They also know that there are continuous changes happening in our planet and other part of universe. In our planet the changes could be attributed to the overuse or misuse of we people with the nature. Scientists evolve new things showing its merit to the mankind. After a decade this innovation starts leading to some sort of disadvantage and so they discover something else to counter the ill effect so envisaged. This way we say to be improving but facing more and more difficult situation ahead. We would keep succeeding to overcome such factors but in saving the future mankind we have already lost of natural species which also were the part of our nature. This is an endless cycle or a cyclic in nature. We are combating the situation of our one earth planet whereas there are infinite stars above us and the changes are taking place continuously which we don't know also.

All this phenomena is not happening haphazardly but is with a great and flawless design.

We human believe in GOD and try to give him/her a shape which we can understand. We being earthly people in 'M' band possess the best wealth to understand in physical language and so different religions have their GOD and it limits to their faith. In 'I' band the understanding would make known of the power which is playing the role and even if a great power like KRISHNA is assumed to be real this GOD call by any such name comes on this earth in that shape. Also it should be understood such GOD who we would understand to be most powerful has a fragment of the total power for controlling our planet. The total power is one which is controlling the entire universe/universe out of our bound of knowledge.

What is this power?

How it is controlling?

The creator has developed the entire universe and is applying some simple rules so that the system keeps functioning. Equilibrium is maintained in totality whereas we having a very short sightness and could see things changing, depleting, vanishing etc., but that is the design to keep the system in equilibrium.

We in scientific terms know that matter cannot be destroyed. It only changes the shape. Matter could be converted into different form and even change in energy but it does not destroy.

What this means to living beings which takes birth and dies. He was born from the matter existing in the (universe) and after the death the matter still remains in the (universe). We have used the word universe because we could be knowing a part which would remain on our planet in the form of earth, water or air but could not be certain of remaining element that gives the meaning of life in the body. *The life giving substance also is constant and could change shape and place but can not diminish.*

This is applicable for all the living being and we human make distinction in species because we have mind and the mind was developed by the creator to evolve and reach to understand the power. We are male or female and this is the first step designed by the creator to generate the duality to maintain equilibrium in this planet. We human have emotions, we are happy and sad, we are greedy and also have sacrificing tendency for others. We are real and we are virtual.

Thus in each part of our existence there is duality spread in the universe for the sake of equilibrium. The understanding does not help us to keep away because of the design of the creator because we are far away to understand the science at the moment.

Operation and Distribution of Power

Further it has been tried to explain the possible method by which 'power' mentioned in the fig. 5.1 governs the system. If we try to understand about the power it could help in reducing the duality in oneself and thus the knowledge could be good for oneself and not possible to globalize for the inherent reason of the design. But such knowledge has to percolate in the appropriate segment who would be the governing to form the upper crust of the pyramid in the fig.5.0.

The science operating for the total equilibrium is similar to the knowledge we know for the material thing. As material is indestructible and can switch in form similarly the noise also generates the waves and remains in existence not to disturb us in physical form.

- Similarly emotions or other characters good and bad such as happiness or sadness are not destroyed.
- Values such as love and hatred, respect and insult are present in a specific amount and can not be eliminated.

What do we mean by this?

The creator has set a specific amount of such *things* and let it play itself in our planet to keep the equilibrium. If I am overhappy or overjoyed for a very long time it could be because of my destiny but by overdoing I am also depriving someone else happiness unknowingly. In other terms if all the ingredients such as happiness, satisfaction, contentment are spread uniformly in all the living beings the planet would be static and there would be no role of the creator in the design. And then the human mind also would not run to find the quest and know the superior designer and thus would be deprived to know about the power which is within him as a seed and could guide to see the source of it.

But it also means that if these ingredient are equally distributed in the living being the positive and the negative aspect would nullify within oneself and the result would be neutral and that is the character of the main source and each segment of the source which is distorted by living being and converted in duality.

The higher knowledge is the one which can bring awareness of the duality and the method to reduce to understand the power source whereas we on the day when we struggle for the different types of the power (physical, political, financial) we tend to keep ourselves in the lower end of the pyramid of the fig. 5.0.

The Operating Power

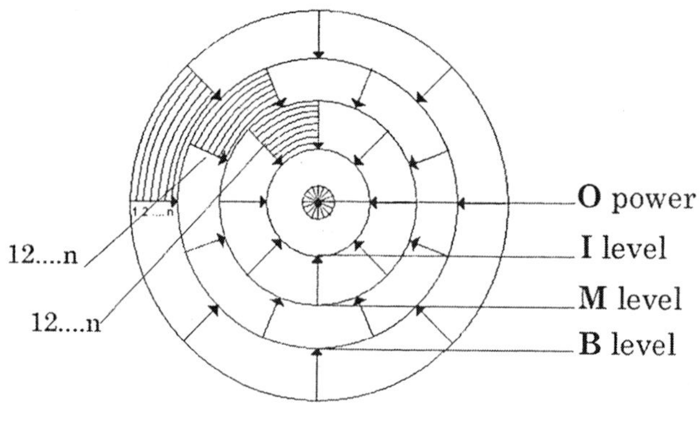

Fig. 5.1

The creator while designing the system has used the tool 'O' in the figure which is invisible power. The invisible power to control our planet is a fraction amount of the whole which similarly is controlling the rest of the universe.

The existence of plants and the mineral we understand very nicely but the behavior with the brain, mind and the intellect of living being has a larger role to play and for us to understand.

In the figure we have

i. Centre point represented by 'O' is the home for the power governing our planet.

ii. Surrounded by circles making segments of I band,

iii. Then M band and

iv. Lastly the B band.

Each band is further subdivided into finer intermediate segments marked as 1, 2, 3 ..... n.

A living being born by his *karma* is placed in any of the points among these bands and he/she has the opportunity to rise a small segment towards the center in one lifetime.

The circle also represents the pyramids structure shown in fig. 5.0 such that near the center the bodies would be lesser in number and as it goes further away the numbers of bodies keep increasing.

'O' is the core or the home of the power and from here it is spread all around covering all the variety of species in the *BRAIN, MIND AND THE INTELLECT BAND. Anyone born in any band would have the seed of power within.* The intensity of the power keeps reducing in the individual identity as one is away from the core vice versa the concentration is more and more as one moves towards the 'I' level.

The power has to balance the total system and it may or may not have the relations with the number of bodies. Each segment is subdivided into infinite subdivisions to show how does power move upwards.

In the beginning if there was only B Band existing it is the band where the cycle moves in natural harmony because of this power. The breeding and habitat of the plant, the breeding and the habitat of the animals belong to this category. The small amount of power imbedded into large volume of bodies allows them to develop specific skills to live at different stages in B band. At this stage distribution of the power has the relation with the number of bodies as well.

Power Home

Core is the home of power. The core is always illuminated and from there it is distributed on the outer periphery such that it reaches and covers all the bands and thus in all the living beings. Total power is constant and a specific amount is distributed in the different bands in all the available bodies of different bands.

The invisible power has the potential to take the living being to the higher level (closer towards the centre) and also has the characteristics to evaporate and rise upwards towards the centre. What this means is that if the body in which power is imbedded does not rise towards the center the power in absence of body would still be attracted towards the home (core).

The movement of the power is in step from its available space towards its home. First it would try to accommodate in the sub-layers of the same band but if it does not get a place in its existing orbit it would move further towards the center.

- For the power existing in 'level B layer-1',let us assume that initially amount of invisible power distributed is 'x' in 'y' number of bodies.
- If the number of bodies in layer 1 of band B are reduced for whatever reason it would try to go up and accommodate in layer-2, 3 and so on.
- In case, the power is unable to find the space in any layer of B band it would travel and find a place in M band and then in I band and
- If still it does not find a place, it would go back to its home (the core).

Power in B band

We would never know but could be that in hard and difficult times the bodies in B Band (which includes all the living beings except human) would be asking the help from GOD to save their bodies!

Who would know it!

And lucky one finding a place in the next band M in

successive births.

B band is followed by the M (Mind) and the I (Intellect) band as a sequential steps to reach the power home that is the core. The power home is the place from where one can directly see and talk with the creator.

To open the channel to reach the core the creator has tapped a small amount of mind. But the process to reach devised is not so simple. Introduction of a small amount of mind has immediately and automatically started destruction of the bodies in the B band generating the superiority. It is the generation of the duality which is also destructing self to understand even if the basic seed (power) of the superior grade has been poured at birth. May be at the last levels of B band and some extraordinary good *karmas* have enabled to evolve in M band but the path is too far to reach'O'.

The power in M band

The characteristic of the power slightly changes here and continue to function to keep the total system in balance. If total power is constant now it does not have relation with the number of bodies. The body may cease to exist but the power would not. Entering the M band the human comes in the subject. To start the life every human has the enough seed or the basic elementary power but human is the species which has deviated from the natural law of the equilibrium. The invisible power which is meant to keep the system in balance knows its role and so this human has the capability to inherit more of the power and also be devoid of the minimum.

There are two types of *karmas* (deeds) affecting human.

- Negative deed (*Ku-karma*) which works to devoid the invisible power and
- Positive deed (*Su-karma*) which allows to accumulate the power.

This devoiding or accumulation of power is not limited in one life and would continue as number of bodies now have no relation further.

In performing negative deeds one throws the available

power and it is only body and mind which appears functioning. It is interesting to know such bodies deprived of the minimum power and could be said to poorer than the animals and go beyond the level of B band entities at time. Any animal infact is proud of his life knows its strength and its ability. Such human performing negative deed looses in the race and looses the opportunity to know his self profound ability to reach the invisible power.

The *ku-karma* performer would be a body and the mind system and for him it would be simple to hurt, kill many bodies without the slightest pain to oneself.

What it cannot do is that he cannot touch the invisible power. The power from such bodies would again travel either in another body or rise upward towards the core.

Thus it is the positive deeds (*su-karmas*) only that is going to lead towards the home of power.

The invisible power has a single function to keep the system in equilibrium. It has the capability to utilize the body and mind to function, to live a useful life, to think, to observe and even do the miracles. In the process of balancing the system it does not bother for the body and individuals.

What would this mean?

In the case of humans if one misuses or overuses his organ and senses one becomes poorer in power. If one misuses or overuses his mind one is more poorer in the power. Each segment of power lost transfers in another body at a higher level or could merge in the power home. It is a tiny amount of power which has the capability to utilize the body and the mind to make one think and do unlimited adventure. In such case if the power is increased the wonder that it can perform could not be imaginable by an average person at least in the present state of human development. It is beyond the imagination of a person today and if one such person would explain it would appear to be unscientific and unbelievable story.

At any level of M band only those bodies who perform *su-karma* and in the process utilize their body organ senses, internal chemistry and mental synthesis in positive way are responsible for holding such invisible power, accumulate it and transfer it. Only such people are responsible to keep the human and the nature exists. If we isolate such people theoretically for a moment the entire mankind would collapse instantaneously.

It may appear that understanding of positive and negative, good or bad are simple. In fact in the global and free information era it would still be understood as simpler task but we forget to think from an individual's perspective which has a narrower end. In last 20 to 25 years the speed of life has increased tremendously. The hunger of material has also increased accordingly. Whereas earlier the life was slower, the hunger of material was less there were lesser problems as well as requirement for the basic need and living in spite of lesser availability. All sorts of negative elements were present but people were of more compromising attitude could be for the prevailing social set up to live jointly or in larger groups. To keep the harmony in a larger group there was another value of patience which was existing. With larger needs, nuclear living has changed the essential values and more of us have deviated from the path in absence of perfect knowledge of self and the actual goal of (human) life.

The Power Game

Let us take a hypothetical example to understand how the power works and how positive performers are the pillars to hold our world. Say for example 40 years back there were 100 positive doers (*su-karmis*) out of 200 people. These *su-karmis* had enough patience and sacrificing tendencies around apart of other values to influence the segment around. In such case the invisible power was distributed such that one positive doer was able to neutralize negative of two people.

After 40 years with changing of time say 40 positive doers remains out of 200 humans. Thus it would mean that now invisible power of one is neutralizing for another 5 persons. Not necessarily but following a linear path we could say that each of these persons would be having more invisible power and it could be collective power in 40 persons that of 100 persons 40 years back which they could accumulate by their own *su-karmas*. These positive doers are the shock absorber of the society and neutralize the sins of others to maintain the balance. Many of these could be appearing as timid / helpless and useless to their counterpart who are soaked in their material world. *The invisible power thus is doing its work even if the act is being abused by the larger segment poor in such knowledge.*

The physical importance of the power would be known once it gets recognition and it would require some more time in our state of evolution. The transfer of power would continue and at each higher sub-layer of the Mind and Intellect the positive doer would keep reducing in numbers and accumulate power would keep increasing in few of them.

But what does this mean to me?

If I am a positive doer (*su-karmi*) at any stage

- irrespective my body lives for a long or not,
- irrespective I get any physical recognition or not,
- irrespective I appear to do some physical achievement or not,

I am a participant in contributing an additional invisible power in some other body with time to come.

It is in the last stage of the intellect band where one would see the height of negative deeds growing and then a glowing accumulated invisible power would find a lucky body to be known as KRISHNA to neutralize the worst possible on this earth.

Naturally a body full of such invisible power would be glowing and would store all sorts of miracle beyond of our scope of imagination. Such glowing power would be detached with his physical body, mind and intellect but the role of physical being would be to use these as a tool to eliminate the climax of sin on earth.

As the power has the potency to keep the system in equilibrium it plays the role in different places as per the requirement.

1. As the intelligent human understands the subject in physical form the power at times has to put in equilibrium by projecting himself in physical form.

2. Even on earth if we consider other matter living or mineral the power would be balancing and communicating to them in the form they understand which could be beyond or understanding. Elimination of species (with respect of the time and situation) and generation of new species (to suit new environment) is the part of this equilibrium played by the power.

3. And there is a world beyond our planet for which very little is known but the power is taking care of that part also.

Limiting our scope of discussion to human and to self and the power which is governing us the advantage of performing positive deeds (*su-karmas*) is that in doing so one is equally responsible in the formation of ultimate glowing body (KRISHNA). This *KRISHNA* is not directly the creator (GOD) but the lucky body who would attain the height of invisible power (power good enough for our planet) and would be in a position to talk to the creator governing the entire universe. He is detached with the body and mind and could live as long as he wishes but he comes with a definite plan to uproot the evil and thus after the job is done has no role to play and shed the body to return merge in the core.

6

ENERGY AND POWER

Self

What a layman can understand by the word power and what could create interest in him?

The laymen could be intelligent re-known person or a poor person who in the very different circumstance with the possession of wealth or in absence of it could be equally disturbed.

i. If the later is forced to starve, former could be asked to starve (medically).

ii. If the former has a higher mind he utilized his energies to accumulate or enjoy the wealth whereas the later could not get the opportunity (due to his placement of his *karmas*).

iii. The former's mental agony is taking a toll on his physical body also whereas the later one is still better as his control over his mind is lower.

This is not to draw any comparison but to indicate that the mental and physical health does not differ much in such two distinct persons which in the social structure would be pole apart. Only if (one such) former person would have cared of one (later person) both would have gained in the whole sum wealth of (invisible) power.

The birth of a human body in specific place and a specific family has a relation with one's own past *karmas* (if one believes) and is not in anybody's control but the act what one does in the present life is important and is bearing in the present life as well.

We have discussed about different mental levels in our earlier chapter and thus the understanding of each has a difference and thus identical effort (good or bad) would make them distinct different humans.

We know the body without mind and soul* is as good as vegetation. Body can create a body and that is how the cycle runs in all the material segments of vegetation, animals and humans. But it is the mind and the soul which differentiates from others and makes us think of a higher governing power.

If this generates the minimum thinking to probe into "self" it should be known and one has not to go very far but all the wealth is in within. We would summarise here how the creator has devised our self system.

Every living being at birth is seeded with a tiny drop of power. This tiny power has the potency to generate energy in the system. The energy is developed through the door of mind/intellect and results in action. The first thing after the birth a doctor or mother wants is the baby to cry and that is the first physical sign of energy bubbling out by the tiny power embedded. This energy makes the baby move his limbs, make noise (a good sign) but after that what happens?

We are busy exhausting our limbs, making noise and much more as we grow and in ignorance of proper knowledge deviate from the path. We destroy the potency of the power within the self and end up being victim of our action physically, mentally, intellectually. The power lost from within escapes in another body or return to the core.

The power is.a neutral thing,

i. it is neither male nor female,

ii. it is neither negative nor positive,

iii. it is neither good nor bad.

The instinct of power to regenerate is governed by love. Below the human level it works in a natural equilibrium but in human it has opened a door.

* *Soul: existence of soul in living body differentiates from vegetation but the power in subject is not the soul. Soul in a body would remain till it lasts but power could increase or decrease according to the utilization. The soul could be said as the seeding power instrument.*

The love understood by human has developed in distinct two following directions,

1. it has generated comparison as the first tool to counter its beauty and
2. has developed logic to become superior.

In the first portion which relates to the value that has helped in the forming an acceptable norm in the developing society it has in the process created all sorts of duality. We are still in the process of evolving and generating many words for the values but the prime word is the first understood as love which we have mastered in destroying as and for our own convenience. The purity of love can be gauged by the unquestioned love between the mother and the child.

The comparison has been the first anti-value subject and led to make the difference of good and bad. Once we have made two posts good and bad with each rise of understanding and addition of meaning love the two posts have been working throughout the evolution. If love is the starting point the end is satisfaction which should be corrected as contentment with basic understanding. The height and the depth of each value has a reference generated from within only.

Ingredients given to living being by the creator:

1. Formost the system runs with two type of living being male and female. One is not enough and that is the first essential place for duality.
2. Sex is primary negative instinct and has a purpose designed by the power. Sex has the relevance to define the parameter for the ultimate pleasure and ultimate

pain.

3 In the natural design the height of pleasure could be felt by male and the height of pain could be felt by female. And in the process the height of pleasure if assumed by female could be an arbitrary whereas the height of pain if gauged by male could be similarly arbitrary.

4 The food for the body is the primary positive values given. The good and enough food has allowed thinking over the other issues including understanding the self in attempt to understand the power within. Living being has moved up in the ladder for this reason only.

5 With time and evolvement the food for body has been the source of food for thought and one would understood that so little actually is required for his body.

The food of thought has developed the logic whereas the logic has allowed to develop science. The science has improved our way of living, allowed to change our thinking but has also activated to generate the superiority within us and beyond us and create a barrier.

Human is fighting against human.

For what?

Superiority.

Over whom?

It is a self professed word one who thinks is leading others politically, financially or any other way.

In the advance stage of our evolution we see the duality in each and every step and the starting point is within and the reason is only self and none other. It is irony that in the age of free information availability

i. Instead of becoming more intelligent we are becoming more ignorant about ourself.

ii. Instead of constructing we are destructing the self.

The progress in science has made reach to the new heights of knowledge of material. It is the design of the power and non-returnable path of progress. Though the science application would continue for betterment of life in all the aspects and can improve the lifestyle by itself it can generate the satisfaction but not the contentment. The science attempts to prove before accepting anything and thus limits its approach to whatever physically can be observed. The mind thought about the freedom of bird in the sky and invented aeroplane but it could not make himself fly which could have given the required freedom. He could make a physical piece of item certainly very useful in globalization but does benefit a very small community of the world. Even if we ask the views for making the aircraft the inventor could have achieved the satisfaction for the good feat and by the effort one has put into it but he would still feel that still we have to work harder so that each one of else could fly themselves.

As the positive energy of some could make the aeroplane the power within can make him fly also.

The fruit of science does not answer the question of duality but does add the burden on consuming the energy.

Energy

Let us understand the energy.

Body

Physical action / movement of any part of the body would require energy. We have to eat, we have to walk, we have to run, we have to hear, we have to see and we have to talk. In short we would use all our body parts to different levels.

Organ

The body parts such as heart, kidney, liver have a specific function and for performing the function the energy is required.

Senses

The action of body and the organs generate the senses. By senses we gauge the difference in beauty or ugliness, sweet or sour, loud or soft, happy or sad. Acknowledging these senses also require energy.

Energy is required in each and every function we do?

We think that energy comes from the food we eat but that is the half fact. Once we eat the food there is a long chain of reaction taking place internally and lot of energy is consumed before certain energy required for external organs could be generated. In modern living with external organs appearing fit we also know that people have different physical ailments which correspond to different functioning of internal organs. We think that because of the advanced medical science we are able to diagnose the ailment. Yes that is true but our knowledge is limited to its physical functioning and the remedy is the replenishment of deficiency physically. We donot know the root cause because the cause is not constant and is related to infinite variables of one's lifestyle.

Lifestyle is a function of mind (and anti-mind) which a doctor would not know but the self would be in a better state to know about it. If mind (and anti-mind) is the cause of the movement of an external organ it is also governing the functioning of internal organs. The advanced human would like to be happy or satisfied without knowing the end goal, these emotions generated also require energy.

If everything we do requires energy how do we know, how much we have and how much has to be consumed. It would be different for different persons and there would be no single method to tabulate it.

In absence of specific knowledge we can certainly think to conserve as much as possible and minimize the waste and for that we go back to the ingredients we mentioned above,

i. External organs: if we are soft with the external organs we would minimize the waste of energy. We should remember the equation P +M =1 of the chapter 2 and in this person situated in the level of equation would require a typical blend of physical and mental energy but if he follows the principle it would elevate his level to understand the self which would keep varying.

ii. Internal organs: start with the food. The right amount and the right quality of the food is the correct choice. The food requirement would follow his mental level but with knowledge and rising mental level the refinement in quality would be known to a specific person rather than a doctor. A specific nutrient diet subscribed can never be perfect for all but today it has become a fashion to follow which is not correct. As we go up in the ladder of mental level the food requirement becomes softer (easily digestible) and lesser in quantity but requires the understanding of utilization (action).

iii. Mental synthesis: Mind and anti-mind are contributing directly or indirectly right from the childhood as we read, write and are learning the life. Mind and anti-mind is teaching to share the happiness or snatch it for the hunger of material, spreading the love or greed within and around. These positive and negative things being operated by our mind and anti-mind also consuming energy. A balance mental frame is a state where minimum energy would be required and thus it is anti-mind which consumes more energy directly and indirectly. Positive deed would consume the minimum energy.

What is the source of continuous energy?

What has role of power to generate energy?

Human has knowledge of different minerals existing in our planet. These minerals are the combination of elements generated by different reactions in certain conducive conditions for its formation. It is the reaction in the presence of combination of chemicals and the energy source which could be in the form of temperature or pressure and time which converts into the new form. In advance technology it is well known that certain reactions at high temperature or pressure or the combination in the presence of catalyst undergo changes which is not possible otherwise. The catalyst in such a case is generally from the family of noble metal (pure metal) and the catalyst by definition means which activates the reaction without any transformation in itself.

Similar is the state in our body where the power within is the catalyst and with the heat and the air does produce the energy with minimum effort. The food source we eat does provide the basic chemical for the reaction to convert into the required energy. The food we eat in absence of power or in lack of power would make the reactions where the energy generated would be unbalanced for the body and thus

i. if generated more would require to be eliminated (and thus cause disturbance) in the mind.
ii. if generated less the mind would still be disturbed.

And along with this there would be side reactions taking place generating toxins for more problems for the body.

When the power within becomes purer or stronger (the state is like a noble metal) it would require minimum effort and minimum food to generate sufficient energy and with minimum side reactions in a steady state of mind. In such state one would know actually how much the body requires and what material is good to generate the required energy and also would know the effort his body has to make to get the required work done using his minimum energy.

We have explained in details about the equation P+M=1 where a balanced work of physical and mental nature per day could make a mind symmetric but in doing so one would keep elevating in mental level and thus would require the changes in his pattern. Nothing is constant and thus one has to be knowledgeable about changes that need to be brought within. This is applicable in M band when mind and anti-mind both are into the action within.

All this knowledge would appear useless when one sees the power which has much more capability than working for the energy. The power has the capability to know or do the things which are physically not possible or seen. So it is important to know a method by which one could make an effort to see the invisible power.

It is the process of evolution that the human would start knowing gradually about the invisible power and then would also know much more as good as miracle as on the day. The power is also helping to catalyses the body energy and if the energy is unbalanced or overused or underused there is enough burden on the body and the mind to keep away from the knowledge of the invisible power.

Hence the first step is necessarily to conserve the energy and produce as much required. But what does this means?

i. Using body organs and senses to the optimum level. How? Do not strain hands, legs, ears, mouth, stomach etc.

ii. Eating fresh and digestible food (which could vary with the area, availability and the individual mental level).

iii. Try to minimize the anti-mind. In the M band the anti-mind has to exist but the knowledge about it could activate to minimize it. Positive deeds are one powerful weapon to win over it. Positive deeds could automatically make the former two points work in automatic harmony.

The sequence of power to operate the universe

We human have limited knowledge to understand the facts in physical form as on the day when we are placed in the M band. Further with evolution we would transfer into the Intellect (I) band which is again the zone of duality. Following the fig. 5.0, structure the rulers would belong to the evolved band but lesser than the former band. The limitation of such evolved person would be the transformed mental knowledge apart of having the physical or the man-made powers. That is the reason a great power source like Krishna or Rama has to come down in our planet for the necessary reform when the evil has piled up. The sequence of the power working is as below,

i. There is a source which is organizing the movement and to keep it in necessary equilibrium of the universe.

ii. One small fraction of this power is taking care for the equilibrium of our planet.

iii. Of this fraction a small portion is embedded as a seed in all the living being.

The one who sows the seed properly by his effort in one's

knowledge or purely by the trust on the power allows it to grow to understand it better and such person is also the savior for the mankind.

The role of power is not only limited within the body but also beyond it and thus if one understands the power he is helping to save our planet in more than the ways we could understand. One can utilize the power to activate another power far beyond the physical reach in many ways and we human in M level would never be able to prove by the present scientific tool for such phenomena. Whereas another living being who trusts the power and his sole job is to help the mankind or the planet and does not bother to prove. He is one who with time would contribute his power in saving our planet. Contribution of power of such noble souls merge to form a body full of glowing power with a name of Krishna the ultimate savior of the mankind in our planet. One need not prove it because even if he is physically responsible for one small act he knows that it is not HE but the power which does not belong to anybody. He is only able to understand or recognize it is due to his nature that has been developed with time and lot of personal efforts which gives a bigger personal joy not understood by any layman.

The Goal of the Life

Today we have human living in distinct two sides which are poles apart.

1. One very educated knowledgeably aware type and
2. Poor deprived of minimum basic necessity.

The major living beings are in between these groups.

Irrespective of one's placement the goal for everyone would be to have a healthy life and with happiness. Both these ingredients if health and happiness are relative and we tend to find outside ourself whereas the answer is within. We keep making a web around our mind and get engrossed in the duality and thus generate the anti-mind such that we keep going away from the goal. In other words the seed power within has been working to generate energy and is being wasted by different outlets of physical and mental means and thus reducing the strength of the power within. If one develops a nature by which one can grow the power within one would know the meaning of healthy life (with minimum requirement on self) and the meaning of happiness or contentment (which would give joy to everyone around).

The nature is dynamic and so the evolving of self is dynamic and so the quest of invisible would be always dynamic and to work it in the positive direction one has to understand the role of power and allow it to percolate to others with time in good souls.

Understanding the power and using for the self-benefit

Majority of people lies in the M band at different levels and thus their behavior and understanding are different. If the understanding of the power is inculcated it could lift oneself in the mental level and thus nullifying the complexity automatically. One should know that,

i. Everyone has the seed power with same capability without any distinction of any class or creed.

ii. Understanding of person at different level requires different technique which is very much available within them.

iii. Power is neutral. It is energy which is negative and positive. Excess usage of either would keep away from the knowledge of power.

iv. With proper utilization of energy and without the knowledge of the power it would make the external and internal circumstances suitable for the self.

v. The dilution of power would allow it to go out of oneself as it's work is to keep the system and is not concern with any individual body.

vi. The power is not the God we understand by any name. The God is a body which is full of glowing power (required for a specific location) to set the rule right. If Rama or Krishna had taken birth on the planet they would take again and they would be carrying the portion of power required to nullify the evil.

vii. The total power is much more in size and capability which is taking care of entire universe and does not have any shape or could form in any shape.

If God is understood as an invisible source which could guide one, the God is one which is full of power only. But the same power in fractional amount is well within us or our people which can be seen and understood physically. It is at the higher level of understanding one would understand the best knowledge and guidance is only within but larger section would try to find outside. In difficult times one tries to seek the guidance and for that one goes in a shelter whom one trusts most and if the trust is strong one gets the relief also. The guide or the guru could be one's parents, friend, a teacher or any preacher.

If one finds relief by parents for him his parents are God and if one finds relief by any spiritual guru he is the God for him. That is why we see so many spiritual gurus coming in picture to cater the major segment of middle class. It is the self-discipline which is the cause for physical or mental healing and the relief felt by the person. It could be the ego that one could be not able to follow self- discipline but the same discipline works when an outsider orders/instructs and one follows it. The self has to continuously evolved and in such case the guru can only help to reduce the negativity and give the relief which is temporary. From this point if one has to keep satisfied physically, mentally the requirement for the discipline would require modification and such guidelines can only emerge from within.

Ideally if one does not waste the energy one would be able to see the power and make it work to do anything but a living being has to use energy for the basic purpose of living. As the end objective is not to become immortal the healthy and satisfied living requires reducing the wastage of energy. In absence of knowledge the body is full of negative energy for which cutting down the negativity is by neutralizing it by positive or reducing the wastage.

Interpretation for reducing the wastage can be understood by an example of observing any one sense say speech.

How much one speaks in a day?

Or how much extra one speaks per day?

One would find out that if he could have spoken 50% less and more effectively the desired communication could have still been completed. Speaking hard and harsh not only is involving physical energy but is also eating the mental energy and in such situation self is going far away from the basic understanding of the power. More people exerting more energy is the fashion and thus the power is eloping from them but is very much there to balance not visible. On the other hand there would be handful of person accumulating the power in the form of patience and tolerance they have been bearing in reformation of others but in today's world they would not be recognized. The accumulated power one day would generate a big soul that would do a big humanitarian job that would be recognized inspite of his requirement.

We are in M band where duality can be reduced by reducing the anti-mind but next the evolved self is going to enter the 'I' band which is also a duality zone and where anti-intellect then designed would be required to be reduced. The 'I' band is not being described in length as we are far from that level on the day and the subject would not make much sense with the present understanding of the people.

All human are born in different levels because of their own *karmas* and so everyone of them is not supposed to understand and rise in the mental level but each one would like to be satisfied in his own conditions. It would be one's own *karma* that he would come across a helping hand with the required knowledge which is able to percolate in his conducive mind at that moment. He would not know much about the elevation of mental level but the process which could give him satisfaction and keep him healthy would help many around him to live so.

- The best of the health does not come only by the food

and living behavior but the understanding of self and self requirement and

- A better understanding would come if conserving the energy is made in the self in some form.
- And conservation of energy (could be very small part) could be understood by everyone in his context of living.

Short Cut To Power

We have described the behavior of mental evolution that is happening and the process by which one day the evolved species of human would be very near to the power source (the creator) or would be going miles apart from him again because of whose evil doing the creator will have to step himself to uproot the evil. It is also described that in the ladder of evolution we have to cross over more than one-third of the height. We are existing in the midst of M band; the evolvement has to cross over M band and then after has to cross over another higher I band. There is another level above Intellect band which we have spelled in the essay without any elaboration which is spiritual band. The spiritual band is important to be included because this band irrespective of any evolution is being experienced by individuals in every corner of our world. It is a short cut for peace which people have been experiencing since ages at the individual level. Anywhere in the world and of any living standard and lifestyle there are people who are devoted lot to the GOD without knowing about the technicality of the power. The dedication towards the GOD in their own way has been giving them a solace and contentment in this material world. Rich peoples belong to this category and poor peoples also belong to this category. If power is the source of the being and is present in everyone which in absence of any adulteration of knowledge is trusted as GOD the same power takes care of that individual which is in his nature.

In the logical way we are far below in the evolution process but we also know that it is the love ingredient of the mind which has changed the process. This love and trust for the creator is the short cut. The trust and dedication towards him (GOD) could be in any form, in any shape because these individual do not contribute directly in the hierarchy of evolution for simple reason that they are far ahead than others. They are not here to make anybody understand but have a focused mind, intellect and much more without the knowledge of these plain words. They are soaked in love and trust with GOD or power and are finding infinite happiness known as bliss. This is to say that spiritual band is the short cut and could be reached directly from any segment in M and I band.

In the progression of M level to I level to S level the utilization of energies and power are optimized.

HOW?

The mind faculty is in the head and operation in M plane is governed from this area. Human understanding from this plane is in three dimension of x, y and z. Whereas in 'I' plane one shifts from the base of mind in head and starts having the knowledge of additional dimension of time. The shift is towards the heart and for that reason the changes in the surroundings (climatic, noise, light or any other) are felt in the heart and conveyed to the mind (which one calls as extra senses). If in 'M' band he was struggling between mind and anti-mind, in 'I' band he would oscillate between mind and heart and cause would be affected with duality of different nature.

It is in S plane the operating is from the seat of heart where nothing in this world could disturb one as whatever one is doing it is effortless work from energy point of view and is very closer to the understanding of power one could reach as the ultimate in our planet.

If in the normal evolutionary process man would be coming closer to the power or going away from him the creator for his satisfaction has made individuals who know the true meaning of love and unquestioned trust and he is the direct care taker of such people. These people are capable to know the ultimate truth which a body and soul system of human can know about maximum.

7

Hypotheses Interpretation And Gita Shlokas

The hypothesis written above was all on the basis of self understanding and the knowledge acquired by experience in the life without reading any of the books on such subject. The subject has relevance with the book published "**The Evolving Human And The Future World**" where the description is of the human mind and its interrelation with other human being. It gives the methodology of the mental development leading to the development of changes in the social structure and the possible route for the future growth. The present subject has been the interpolation of the same with the description of changes in self which is the ultimate ruler at the first point. A king could be a recognized personality in his kingdom loved and respected by his authoritative nature or his good deeds. The king known due to his good deeds has been able to set some rules acceptable to all for the constructive growth of a larger mankind. Similarly everyone is the king on his own body and mind system and the king among these who have set a rule for a larger mankind are the true constructors of the mankind at any part of the evolution. Mahatma Gandhi can be termed as one for example who utilized the self power to expand much beyond his limit for a good cause of a larger humanity at the prevailing time and circumstance.

After completing the hypotheses the author has read a few books of philosophy such as,

Bhagavad-Gita, As It Is *by Swami Prabhupada,*

Ramayana *by Kamal Subramanyam,*

Autobiography of a Yogi *by Paramhansa Yogananda*

All these books have strengthen the view of author on the power mentioned in the concept and also strengthens the developmental behavior in M band which is presently prevailing and then to the 'I' band which has to follow with time to come.

"*Autobiography of a Yogi*" by Paramhansa Yogananda is the live example in our age of a man who had reached 'I' level and 'S'. The book describes the knowledge of the power as mystic power and also the difference between two such people one who uses mystic power to reduce the power within to amalgamate with the actual power and reach 'S' level and one who has merged in 'S' band has a control beyond the physical body for the welfare of the nature and human community. There would be plenty who are secluded and unknown but their present status calls to be away from any human disturbance which the world is full of in the present time. The knowledge could be known by mass only when the evolutionary process would reach there and some are recognized with time.

Bhagavad-Gita and *Ramayana* are the scriptures of Hindu religion and people read and teach it as a faith. Some may see these as a story line which could have taken place or not. Terming them as philosophy the matter ends. Does such philosophy have much relevance today? Have we developed with the help of scientific understanding?

The science is validated by the truth of proving in physical level. And we owe our better standard of lifestyle and understanding to the science only. Science has been able to develop man-made superior aids for constructing and destructing nature and the mankind. What is important to know is that we are at present in M band of evolution and the best a human can develop would be man-made thing which could be termed a physical thing. There would be a time when human would enter the I band which has the power of mental strength against physical strength. That time the present technology man-made things would exist and science would crawl behind and try to prove certain things also but it would always remain behind the actual heights and depth which power is able to cope with.

Thus the philosophy becomes the base level of science followed by certain brains to work on specific ideas and build a hypothesis. Science gives a useful outcome to be understood with explanation to a mortal human when worked continuation on the hypothesis. The author feels that the philosophy mentioned in the epic such as *Gita* and *Ramayana* are very much the facts which are happening and describes the outcome which we human would continue to face tomorrow.

We have discussed different levels in the process of evolution namely :

1. Brain level,
2. Mental level,
3. Intellectual level,
4. Is followed by spiritual level which we have not spoken about.

Accordingly the different planes one comes across are as follows:

1. At the brain level there is a natural equilibrium of the total state.
2. At the mental level physical plane comes in picture where every scientific development is of physical nature. Attraction and hatred is of physical nature and all that is for by the development of mind and anti-mind. This could be understood by any person.
3. At the intellect level (which is yet to come) the anti-mind has been won and so physical plane is crossed and one enters mental plane. Here the type of nature would be

similar to the physical plane but with a difference where one would be capable to cope with mental strength which one could find difficult to understand as on the day.

4. We have not discussed about the fourth as that is a region devoid of any duality and of much higher level and of lesser practical relevance on the day.

The M and I level are with plane of duality which keeps acting to devoid the knowledge of the power. There are innumerable sub-layers in these categorized M and I level and an intelligent person in (elevated) M level would know to communicate with another person in the same level according to his capability of understanding. That is to say he would be able to explain to different persons in the same level in different format by which they can understand the subject.

Similarly an intelligent person in (elevated) I band would have a large cross section of people in M band and also different layers of I band and his communication would demand a wider communicating method to make the subject clear to different cross section of the people.

In *Bhagavad Gita* the major communication between *Krishna* and *Arjuna* is between two persons situated at an elevated intellect level. Therefore the interpretation of the meaning of the shlokas could be different by different persons. There could be a difference in who is communicating and there could be difference in one who is listening. It is only a self who experiences a fraction of it could understand it better for his life.

Bhagavad Gita is not only the philosophy of the life but also the philosophy for the entire evolutionary process and does try to emphasis the struggle of war within by projecting the war outside. It clearly describes about the different mental levels and is not limited to B and M band which we have discussed in length but explains further of I (Intellect) level which we have touched and also spiritual level which we have not touched at all. It is about the war to conquer on oneself to know about the power and for that one has to fight with anti-mind (in M level) to come out of it and then to fight with anti-intellect (in I level) to meet with the power face to face.

Bhagavad Gita could be immortal epic applicable at all times of the mankind in yester age, present age and with age to come and interpretation of the subject could lead to misinterpretation of the actual essence and so the author can not think of himself capable of doing so. However the author has tried to selectively explain certain shlokas of "*Bhagavad Gita*" which finds relevance to the concept or the hypothesis which is based for the evolution stage of human today with the extrapolation mentioned of future. Author has also tried to explain how the meaning would vary with the difference between or within M and I levels.

Chapter 1 shloka 48

Yoga-stha kuru karmani sangam tyaktva dhananjaya
Siddhy-asiddhyoh sama bhutava samatvam yoga ucyate

Perform your duty equipoised, O Arjuna, abandoning all attachment to success or failure. Such equanimity is called yoga.

Yoga is defined here as a composure where one is in complete self-control of mind. Whereas our hypotheses describes about a balanced mental frame which can be attained by balancing P+ M=1 in M level. This equation would be different for all according to their state. It is a method by which temporarily anti-mind is kept away. Similarly the requirement in the I band which is not discussed in the book would be a sum of P+M+I=1 and would have same end meaning to keep away the anti –intellect temporarily.

If one can make or remove anti-mind in M band whatever he does in action would be meeting yoga requirement and for that one shall be ready to face the ups and down in the life with calm posture which are part and parcel of the life.

Chapter 2 shloka 52

Yada te moha-kalilam buddhir vyatitarityati

Tada gantasi nirvedam srotavyasya srtuasya ca

When your intelligence has passed out of the dense forest of dilution, you shall become indifferent to all that has been heard and all that is to be heard.

- The M band where we are situated is full of duality and once we overcome it we would land in I band which is different and situated at higher level. This I band is also the region of duality where using and abusing of physical powers are overcome but using and abusing of mental powers become prominent. The shloka describes and says that if you cross over the I band or have conquered the duality of I band you would enter the spiritual band which does not have duality and is pure and would make understanding of the governing power within.

The description is further elaborated in shloka 55 more about spiritual band (beyond I band). Nevertheless it would make sense in the extrapolation of our hypothesis. The wordings are,

Chapter 2 shloka 55

Prajahati yada Kaman sarvan partha mano-gatan
Dtmany evatmana tushah sthita-prajnas tadocyate

O *Partha (Arjun)*, when a man gives up all varieties of desire for the sense of gratification, which arise from mental concoction, and when his mind, thus purified, finds satisfaction in the self alone, then he is said to be in pure transcendental consciousness (which is spiritual band).

Chapter 2 shloka 60

Yatato hy api kaunteya purusaya vipascitah
Indriyani pramathini haranti prasadabham manah

O *Arjun*, the senses are so strong and impulsive that they forcibly carry away the mind even of a man of discrimination who is endeavoring to control them.

- Reduction of anti-mind and anti-intellect is difficult

(not impossible) is described here. That is why the evolution is in a pyramid shape and lesser and lesser living being would rise towards that but the evolution process towards that is inevitable and so the quest would continue to know about the power or the power source.

Chapter 3 (*Karam yoga*) the content of this chapter could be useful for entire mental band but has more relevance for the people today and could be better understood whereas the chapter 2 was for the higher mental level.

Chapter 3 shloka 16

Evam pravartitam cakram namuvartayatiha yah
Aghayur indriyaramo mogham partha sa jivati

O *Arjun*, one who does not follow in human life the cycle of sacrifice thus established by the vedas certainly, leads a life full of sin. Living only for the satisfaction of the senses, such a person lives in vain.

- The verses in this chapter have described the sacrifices of different type applicable for different mental levels and sub-levels. This verse describes the importance of sacrifice to rise in the mental level. The simplest and the basic understanding of sacrifice at the lowest level is reducing the wastage of energy and the primary method described is to cut down the wastage of BOS, IBC and MS which can be identified by any individual.

At very lower level of B band one's requirement would be more physical activity and lesser activity and even if a person gets an opportunity for work he would be unable to judge for the mental portion and would simply talk more or crude to others whereas if he would have restrain in his thought that would be also a small sacrifice. At higher B band restrain in physical activity for projecting one's position would be the sacrifice. Charity or helping others at the cost of own comfort could be understood. If I have anything in plenty, distributing to the needy would be good but not sacrifice because sacrifice is associated with the intention which is pure form the self as between mother and her child which may or may not involve in any material. A person could be following a path of value in his knowledge not hurting anybody else in anyway but could be still finding many obstacles in his life. If such person oversees and does not compare anyone else who could be having much lesser obstacles irrespective of his negative path the former who finds the obstacles is the sacrifice (without one's knowledge).

Such sacrifice is the cleansing solution for a person of his sins past or present and helps in removing the anti-mind and or anti-intellect to purify him and reach closer to the power.

Chapter 3 shloka 35

Sreyan sva dharmo vigunah para-dharmat sv-anusthitat
Sva-dharme nidhanam sreyah para-dharmo bhayavahah

It is far better to discharge one's prescribed duties, even though faultily, than another's duty perfectly. Destruction in the course of performing one's own duty is better than engaging in another's duties to follow another's path is dangerous.

- This verse describes about the ego in a self which is the cause of destruction for elevating oneself. The perception of one being bigger or higher in material or even knowledge is self believe and is when he compares to the other people around and judges himself for the results which itself has a flaw. A true honest to oneself person would never judge but would only put his point of view on any matter. This does not mean that in work one should not take any decision but if the decision taken honestly would not matter because results in any circumstances could be good or bad. An honest decision keeps the situation alive to modify reform without harming anyone. It is the ego that forces oneself to demand rather than command and create larger anti-mind causing the slower elevation towards the power.

Chapter 3 shloka 38

Dhumenavriyate vahnir yathadarso malena ca

Yatholbenavrto garbhas tatha tenedam avartam

As fire is covered by smoke, as mirror is covered by dust or as the embryo is covered by the womb similarly the living entity is covered by different degrees of the lust.

- This verse describes the very nature of the living entity and the duality in mind and intellect band. If there was no anti-mind there would not have been any progression in the life and that is the rule of the power. The one who conquers the anti-mind and anti-intellect is one who is capable to understand about it and make progress towards it.

Chapter 3 shloka 40

Indriyani mano buddhir asyadhisthanam uchyate
Etair vimohayaty esa jnam avrtya dehinam

The senses, the mind and the intelligence are the sitting places of the lust. Through them lust covers the real knowledge of the living entity and bewilders him.

- the whole design of the power was to filter out the living entity and make the purest to reach in a position to understand him. BOS, IBC and MS are the tools in the M band to cross over the anti-mind by putting restrain whereas mind itself becomes the tool and requires restrain in I band ahead.

Chapter 3 shloka 42

I indriyani parany ahur indriyebhah param manah
Mansas tu para buddhir yo buddheh paratas tu sah

The senses are said to be superior, the mind is higher than the senses, intelligence is still higher than the mind and the power is even higher than the intelligence.

- The verse describes the process of power and it is gradual. If everyone was to reach and understand very easily the purpose of the design would have been defeated. In that perspective it is said that senses are superior as they are the gates to understand and reach the power. It also says that mind is superior and intelligence is still superior as we have described in the hypothesis.

Chapter 4 shloka 06

Ajo pi sann avyayatma bhutanam isvaro pi san
Prakrtim svam adhisthaya sambhavamy atma mayaya

Although I am unborn and my transcendental body never deteriorates and although I am the lord of all living entities I still appear in every millennium in my original transcendental form.

- The verse describes about the whole power which is planning the design for the entire universe. The lord says that he is the power for controlling the entire system and of that one small part is good enough to control our planet. He further says that he comes in the form of human with all that glowing power to balance the grown evil to bring back the equilibrium. It is the power of living entity that is making the human body in different times and in different forms. If *Krishna* would be the ultimate body for the ultimate reform the same power at the intermediate level develops person like *Mahatma Gandhi* (to name one) who commands a big segment for a noble cause of the people.

Chapter 5 shloka 04

Sanhya-yogau pratag balah pravdaanti na panditah
Ekam apy asthitah samyag ubhayor vindate phalam

The less intelligent people differentiate between the analytical study and the devotional service. Those who are actually learned say that he who applies himself well to one of these paths achieves the results of both.

This verse has a larger meaning on human evolution. It is the values and logic sense which has allowed human to improve upon and make us reach to the point where we exist. If the values have been the bonding force for the human agglomeration under different heads such as family, society, nation etc. it has been the logic sense which has improved the skills that has developed man-made resources to achieve what could never have been imagined. At present (in M band) the logics have aided to facilitate different man-made things which are of physical nature and same logic sense (in I band) would make development of mental nature as well. The balanced understanding of a person is when his understanding of values matches with the logic sense (which has been described in the book "The Evolving Human And The Future World") and that is also essential for the mental growth. Such person or even the leader who can match these two elements would be said to have reduced the anti-mind which is the requirement for the self. It indirectly would take care of the ingredients for serving others, having sacrificing tendencies for a larger human cause and resilience in the decisions taken. One who works in dedication for the larger cause (with minimum anti-mind) would understand that both the value and analytical approach are two sides of the same coin.

Chapter 5 shloka 05

Yat sankhyaih prapyate sthanam tad yogair api gamyate
Ekam sankhyam ca yah pasyati sa pasyati

One who knows that the position reached by means of analytical study can also be attained by devotional service and who therefore sees analytical study and devotional service to be on the same level see things as they are.

- Analytical study is logic sense (or the science) is again related to the devotional service which is value. The core value is love and one loves the self and understands the real meaning of such love does spread only love around. Such a person would be making a devotional service to the power in the spiritual level. In the M band core value of love remains the same but is mixed up with its extension fins of physical nature and with the existing evolved pattern the love has more fins such as respect, moral values and humanity. Understanding of each successive word (which means the same 'love' for all) requires elevating the logic sense. Persons at any level of M and I who have a balanced level of value and logic sense are the persons with minimum negativity and their perspective for anything is in harmony. They are the leaders in the evolution irrespective of any kind of recognition. In fact recognition is the barrier in his lifetime nevertheless such human generates few others one of whom would go still higher. In I band the core value of love would have an extended fin of mental nature and the higher logic sense also would be attached with the mental nature. The mental nature in this band would thus keep making the separating the elevation who are trapped with anti-intellect because of its superior gimmick capability. But one who is able to balance the mental power along with physical power would find closer to the actual power source.

The above verse says that the same devotional services and the analytical study leads to the same end and these two things are the main branches for creating the duality which further develops many more sub branches for duality where most of the humans keep getting lost in their path of elevation.

Chapter 5 shloka 8-9

Naiva kincit karomiti yukto manyeta tattva-vit

Pasyan srnavan sprsan jighrann asnam gacchan svapan svasan

Pralapan visrjan grhnann unmisan nimisann api

Indriyanindriyarthesu vartanta iti dharayan

A person in the divine consciousness although engaged in seeing, hearing, touching, smelling, eating, moving about, sleeping, breathing always know within himself that he actually does nothing at all. Because while speaking, breathing, receiving or opening or closing his eyes he always knows that only the material senses are engaged with objects and that he is aloof from them.

- As *Krishna* is speaking the ultimate truth in the *Bhagavad Gita* the essence is much more beyond our immediate subject as it is covering the evolving portion of us as well. We have said that in the existing M band organs and senses are the regions where one looses the energy for various reasons. We have also said that by conservation of the energy one is able to reduce the anti-mind prerequisite for elevating oneself. We have further explained that there are direct overuse of (external and internal) organs and senses which one can reduce in his daily activities which would keep him calm and certify for rising. In I band we have said that mind is in symmetric condition with no anti-mind but the duality is of different nature. If in M band physical organ and senses which we know as over working or under working consume energy in I band mind is the tool which makes the organs and senses move. The energy loss is by the over using and or under using the mind (not the physical organs and senses as they are the tool of mind here). The verse describes the same taking this till one step forward and is the ideal situation to reach the power. When crossing the I band the energy loss due to the mind factor is also over and thus one has stepped in spiritual band. Person at this stage would have conserved the energy so much that he is so closer to the power and in such case whatever the physical or the mental (internal and the external) organs and senses do they do it automatically as per the demand of power and would be purer and refined elevated to understand the seed power within.

Chapter 6 shloka 06

Bandhur atmatmanas tasya yenatmaivatmana jitah

Anatmanus tu satrutve vartetatmaiva satru-vat

For him who has conquered the mind, the mind is the best of friends but for one who has failed to do so his mind will remain the greatest enemy.

- If in the M band the mind and the anti-mind are the reason for generating poison or nectar in one's body resulting the action seen in organs and senses in the I band, mind is still used as an organ to use the organs and senses. The mind in this state becomes as the main physical organ and so keeps its importance directly or indirectly. Accordingly in this verse importance of mind is given and conquering it is vital for evolving.

Chapter 6 shloka 16-17

Nayy-asnatas tu yogosti na caikanatam anasnatah
Na cati-svapana-silasaya jagrato naiva carjuna
Yuktahara-viharasya yukta-cestaya karmasu
Yukta-svapanavabodhasya yogo bhavati duhkha-ha

There is no possibility of one's becoming a yogi. O *Arjun* if one eats too much or too little, sleeps too much or does not sleep enough.

He who is regulated in his habits of eating, sleeping, recreation and work can mitigate all the material pains by practicing the yoga system.

- yoga is the state where upon one can keep away from the mind and anti-mind, intellect and anti-intellect and so strengthen the power within and thus recharge in the physical form. The verse thus explains that one in this body form has to be very much here and do the necessary functions desired by the body. In this body form and by regulating the life one can very much understand the power within. Few probabilities mentioned are related to use the organ and sense optimally describing such as over eating or eating less, over sleeping or sleeping less would take you away from the yogic state. Each part in one's knowledge (external or internal) has to be used in optimum level that is just as much required. This requirement would vary for everyone and would certainly lead to the elevation in understanding of self. In one instance the mind has to be very active (in constructive work) if one is situated around 0.5 M level and in one instance mind's activity has to be reduced when he is near the 1.0 M level. Conservation in wasteful energy and doing the daily work a person in M band can have maximum feeling or the strength of Intellect band whereas a person in I band in a similar situation would start understanding the role of the power which he must have collected in the process.

Chapter 6 shloka 29-30-31

Sarva-bhuta-stham atmanam sarva-bhutani catmani
Iksate yoga-yuktatma sarvatra sama-darsanah

Yo mam pasyati sarvatra sarvam ca mayi pasyati
Tasyham na pranasyami sa ca me na pranasyati

Sarva-bhute-sthitam yo mam bhajaty ekätvam asthitah
Sarvath vartamano pi sa yogi mayi vartate

A true yogi observes Me in all beings and sees every being in Me. Indeed the self-realized person sees Me, the same supreme Lord everywhere.

For one who sees Me everywhere and sees everything in Me, I am never lost, nor is he ever lost to me.

Such a yogi who engages in the worshipful service of the supersoul is one who always remains always in ME in all circumstances.

- *Krishna* has used Me for the power and the *Krishna* which comes to the planet for setting the equilibrium and eliminating the generated excess evil is a small part of power which is operating the entire universe. We have also said that each entity has the seeding power which makes a difference between a living entity and a dead body. Either the power is exhausted through the route of wasteful energy (in most of the cases) or if energy restrain is done power within increases also and thus one rises up in the ladder of evolution. If one has collected more power even if he leaves the body the power is going back in the core (home place). And in the process this person is part of the formation of Krishna. So if the power within is same in all as the power in core centre, there is no difference in characteristics a self-realized person would not differentiate anyone and would love everyone which would be a true yogic state full of contentment.

If one tries to understand the self and the power within which is the catalytic cause for everything one would like to be associated with such knowledge as it would keep him content and make him do the necessary for the function required and such a person would be in a yogic state.

Chapter 7 shloka 4

Bhumir apo 'nalo vayuh kham mano buddhir eva ca
Ahankara itiyam me bhinna prakritir astadha

Earth, water, fire, ether, mind, intelligence and false ego all together these eight constituents are my separated energies.

- This verse clearly describes intelligence as one separate constituent over mind, and false ego in the sequence confirms that intelligence (I band) which is higher than the mind is also a region of duality where false ego would surface. Ego is the highest order of negativity present in the living being. We understand the ego or more precisely false ego of the mind (as we are situated in M level). I band would also have this component which would work against elevation of self. Further the other constituent mentioned such as earth, air, water, fire, ether are the materials of the body which is the tool for self to understand the power within. There is a larger meaning also that each constituent separately itself has a portion of power and has a mechanism for controlling the equilibrium. We people in the advanced scientific age may not consider earth, water, air and fire more than the support system but mountains, rivers are the life lines for living beings and we do have knowledge of environment and find its degradation as the negative symptoms for living being. As the power is neutral the power in the environment is also neutral. When we disbalance the nature by extracting the positive (as we see a material gain in it) we shift the neutrality and what remains is the negativity which we start fearing for the future.

Chapter 7 shloka 8-9

Raso 'ham apsu kaunteya prabhasmi sasi-suryayoh
Pranavah sarva-vedesu sabdah khe paurusam nrsu

Punyo gandhah pritivyam ca tejas casmi vibhavasau
Jivanam sarva-bhutesu tapas casmi tapasvisu

O son of *Kunti*, I am the taste of water, the light of the sun and the moon, syllable om in the vedic mantra, I am the sound in ether and the ability in a man.

I am the original fragrance of the earth and I am the heat in the fire. I am the life of all that lives and am the penance of all ascetics.

- 'I' is representing *Krishna* in *Gita* and in our hypothesis this is a part of the power that is controlling the system which is again a fragment of the bigger power that is taking care of entire universe/s existing. The power within is catalyzing I self to the mind through which the sensing organs work for taste and smell. The vibration by om has the ability to make a symmetric mental frame and thus is stated as power which could help in controlling the other senses to understand the power within. As power is constant the other ingredient such as happiness and sorrow, gratification and penance are also constant. Happiness and gratification generally any person would like to be associated but if all could possess it where would the other half remain. The other half that is sorrow and penance are still spread on our planet except it could not be seen around or if seen could not be correlated with other beings. Actually in the I band one would have the logical understanding for such correlation between different living beings. One knows it or is unaware the balancing act of nature by the power keeps happening. In M band one is overjoyed and another living being not related elsewhere is suffering would never know but they are contemporary to each other and are balancing each other. In I band penance is used to keep someone happy similarly in one's knowledge and for a good cause. Such is the power of penance mentioned in the verse.

Chapter 7 shloka 10

Balam balavatam caham kama-raga-vivarjitam
Dharmaviruddho bhutesu kamo smi bharatarsabha

I am the strength of the strong, devoid of passion and desire; I am sex life which is not contrary to the principal. O lord of the Bharata.

- the verse clearly states that the physical component of strength is generated from power within but the power is neutral and thus a balanced person can utilize the strength if the source is not exhausted in excess for any other self requirement. Sex is not bad as that is the media planned for regeneration and power within is the cause. We have said in the hypothesis that sex utilizes negative energy and anti-mind is the cause for the temptation. It is essential for living being for the existence but its importance finishes there only. Therefore the sex is said to be a very good reference for understanding the anti-mind and gradually its realization could help reform oneself. Being governed by anti-mind excess in sex could sharply take away from the understanding of power.

Chapter 7 shloka 21-22-23

Yo yo yam yam tanum baktah sraddhayarcitum icchati
Tasya tasyacalam sraddham tam eva vidadhamy aham

Sa taya sraddhaya yuktas tasyaradhnam ihate
Labhate ca tatah Kaman mayaiva vihitan hi tan

Antavat tu phalam tesam tad bhavaty alpa-medhasam
Devan deva-yajo yanti mad-bhakta yanti mam api

When my devotee desires with faith for whichever demigod I make his faith steady so that he can devote himself to that particular deity.

Endowed with such a faith he endeavors to worship a particular demigod and obtains his desire. But in actuality these benefits are bestowed by Me alone.

Men of small intelligence worship the demigods and their fruits are limited and temporary. Those who worship the demigods go to the planets of the demigods but My devotees ultimately reach My supreme planet.

- These verses explain the evolutionary path of the living being. If in the last one we saw the essential role of anti-mind (negative energy) and further we understand the importance of reducing the negative energy could be that one builds up excess of positive energy. Positive energy is the source for elevation in the evolution but excess of this also would mislead and thus mentioned the stage of reaching or understanding demigod and the full power source. We have explained in the earlier chapter that *Krishna* when comes in our planet is one with a fraction of power which is capable of the purpose of balancing the spared evil whereas the total power is one which is controlling the total universe/s. Self in the process would limit to the understanding of *Krishna* (fraction of total power) with excess of positive energy (which would happen in M and I band). In the end of I band when one is reaching towards spiritual "S" band about which the theory is not mentioned one would reduce the excess positive energy and would understand about the actual power and would be able to join the power within to that of the source.

Chapter 9 shloka 10

Mayadhyaksena prakritih suyate sa-caracarm
Hetunanena kaunteya jaga viparivartate

This material nature which is one of My energy is working under My direction, O son of *Kunti* producing all moving and non-moving beings. Under its rule this manifestation is created and annihilated again and again.

- This verse has extended meaning beyond the self. The part of the power is within all the living beings and is also in non-living being (non-moving). If we are able to understand the power within we would be able to understand the power in non-moving things also. The natural balancing strength of this power could be seen in moving and non-moving bodies. The environment changes due to the human excesses is the cause to impact human again for balancing. There are creatures and animals which become extinct due to the specific changed conditions but many new develop to suit the new condition for balancing the act. We human may keep destroying various known bacteria or viruses but new would keep developing to meet the new situation. The role of the power is similar in a self or any other body near or a bigger body far away. We know of black hole where planets and stars enter and stop emitting light. The black hole annihilates stars as we know is the role of power which does due to the situation factor prevailing. Extinction of creature and animals are also annihilation and cropping of newer breed is the creation. Thus explained here is that the role of the power is very big but very simple and is spread everywhere and to understand the simplest is to see within and all the power has the same potential for its action.

Chapter 10 shloka 10-11

Tesam satata-yagtanam bhajatam priti-purvakam
Dadami buddhi-yogam tam yena mam upayanti te

Tesam evanukamparthanı aham ajnana-jam tamah
Nasayamy atma-bhava-stho jnana-dipena bhasvata

To those who are constantly devoted to serving Me with love, I give the understanding by which they can come to Me.

To show them special mercy I dwell in their hearts, destroy with the shining lamp of knowledge the darkness born of ignorance.

- In chapter V "Invisible Power" we have described about the operating power and also informed about the power home. The power at core to keep our planet in equilibrium is fractional in amount of that which is controlling the entire universe system but this fractional power is also too much in itself. We have also said the power within could be gained or lost and whatever is lost evaporates towards the core in higher human or to the power home. Now if *Krishna* is the power source He can be viewed possessing a fractional portion (for governing our planet) or the total power which is governing the entire universe by different person but that is immaterial. The person who gains the power or elevates himself in higher Intellectual and spiritual plane he has to possess a unique nature of neutrality and would be contended and glowing person and to that Lord *Krishna* says in this verse that if one is devoted to me I take care of him which is again the same. The true meaning of love and trust at the elevated plane is what makes the difference.